Why Love Hates Legalism

By Ron Sutton

Unless otherwise indicated, all Scripture quotations are taken from the King James Version (KJV) of the Bible.

Why Love Hates Legalism
ISBN: 978-1501070679
Copyright © 2014 by Ron Sutton

Printed in the United States of America. All rights reserved under International Copyright Law. Contents may not be reproduced in whole or in part in any form without the expressed written consent of the authors, except quotations, or brief passages for use in sermons, articles or reviews.

ABOUT THE AUTHOR

Ron Sutton was converted from a life of crime and drug abuse during the Jesus Movement in 1972. His ministry has taken him to sixty nations. He has conducted mass crusades and leaders' conferences, served as a missionary, evangelist, pastor and church planter. His books on evangelism, gospel tracts and pro-life literature have been distributed throughout the USA and internationally. He and his wife Cindy established a drug rehabilitation ministry, a childrens' home in Costa Rica, and a home for unwed mothers. Ron served for several years as director of the School of Christ International in Africa. He currently continues to travel in ministry, and assist his son Ryan at The Grace Center.

TO ORDER MATERIALS OR SCHEDULE MEETINGS
The Grace Center
P.O. Box 21, Crystal City, Missouri 63019

Phone: 636-465-0885

www.TheGraceCenter.org

Ron Sutton
P.O. Box 2207, Hillsboro MO 63050

www.RonSuttonMinistries.com

Phone: 314-960-8306

CONTENTS

Introduction: An Irreverent Indictment of Mean Religion........7
1. Small-Brained Religion..17
2. The Holy Ghost Made Me Do It................................25
3. Will The Real Holy Ghost Please Stand Up?.................35
4. The Devil Made Him Do It.....................................45
5. Jesus Was Not Nice to the Legalists..........................53
6. This Snake Has Fangs...59
7. Run While You Can..65
8. It's Just Manure, Man..71
9. The Jesus Only Heresy 77
10. The Plurality and the Oneness of the Godhead............93
11. A Little Leaven Contaminated a Lot of Bread............101
12. Get Your Own Converts.......................................109
13. All Hat and No Cowboy..115
14. Apostolic Revivalists or Apostolic Religionists?............131
15. The Serpent Is Subtle...141
16. The Left Foot of Fellowship..................................145
17. A Reputation in Hell..151
18. Violent Love 165
19. Bad Doctrine: The Foundation of Mean Religion........171
20. Loose Lips..177
21. He Couldn't See My Heart for My Hair...................193
22. Religion or Revolution?..201

Introduction

An Irreverent Indictment of Mean religion

Love hates legalism because of what it does to its victims. Legalistic Christianity is mean religion. It continually hurts vulnerable believers, especially new ones. The spirits behind the legalistic religious systems I address in this book are the same ones that stirred up a mob in Jerusalem 2000 years ago to cry, "Crucify Him! Crucify Him!" They are still with us in 2014, hiding behind a myriad of religious masks. The masks often don't come off until they are forced to step out of the dark shadows of mean religion. Jesus deliberately provoked the Pharisees and Paul provoked the Judaizers to this end: They drew them out of the shadows of religion, into the light of authentic Christianity, in order to expose their shallowness and hypocrisy.

In the following pages, I transparently share some of the trouble and pain legalistic Christians have caused me throughout the course of over forty years of ministry. I realize that some will read and think I am bitter, using this book as a vehicle to vent my feelings. Hopefully at my age, painful dealings with legalists all over the world have made me better and not bitter. I am not assaulting the foreboding walls of Christian legalism to vent bitterness or anger. I do so in the hope that modern Judaizers might see the light, and that victims of legalistic religious systems might find freedom in Christ. When I speak of legalism, I am referring to narrow-minded doctrinal systems that emphasize works, frustrate grace, and insist on strict adherence to religious rules and unreasonable codes of dress and conduct.

I make no apology for not being politically correct. Some will consider me mean-spirited because I challenge legalism forcefully. That would be a small price to pay if even one prisoner of mean religion finds the exit sign and enters the liberty of authentic Christianity.

From the earliest days of my ministry in the Jesus Movement in 1973, mean religion has dogged my trail throughout the world. I have encountered legalism masquerading as holiness in the USA, Latin America, Europe, Africa and Asia. It has caused me trouble among pastors and churches who previously had cooperated together to plan crusades and conferences. I have been ambushed by Apostolic Revivalists who would have been more appropriately called Apostolic Religionists. Their insidious influence has often produced strife and division where before there had been unity and cooperation. Experiences too numerous to discuss here have left me with little tolerance for legalists who, unable to win their own converts, try to steal them from others. They mingle with new believers won by others in order to make proselytes. I have watched the joy of many of those new believers dissipate as modern Pharisees trap them and weigh them down with dogmatic doctrines and ridiculous dress codes.

I make no apology for the irreverence I show for legalistic religious systems in this book. Legalism hurts people Jesus loves. It binds people Jesus desires to set free. I believe myself to be in good company: Jesus and all the Apostles, with the possible exception of James and his "Judaizing" friends, had the same sentiment: They loved those bound by legalism but they hated the spirit of narrow-minded, mean religion. I am not declaring war on any person. My warfare is not with flesh and blood. It is with the religious spirits that drive the legalistic organizations to which they are attached.

Am I mad? No. I am in complete control of my words and my emotions. Everything you read, if you choose to continue, is calculated and deliberate. By the time your eyes fall on these pages, I will have read and re-read them countless times. Nothing that remains will have escaped my scrutiny. I will have no regrets, nor apologies, for any word or phrase that follows. This is a deliberate, in-your-face, affront to religion that imprisons people with rigid doctrines and unreasonable codes of dress and behavior. What you may perceive as crass or crude comments are not in these pages by accident or oversight. I deem them an appropriate response to mean religion that is too often given a pass; it is given a pass because confrontation is nearly a lost art in many of the polite, passive churches of America.

I have watched too many new Christians lose all their peace after an encounter at an altar with Mr. Legalist. I am sickened at the thought of countless converts who lost their new found joy in the Lord because a legalistic Judaizer told them they were not saved until they had been baptized with the right formula, or until they had spoken in other tongues. I am weary of sermons about the sin of long hair on men, short hair on women, and ridiculous dress codes that embarrass and humiliate youth who are subjected to them. I have had my fill of the jewelry and make-up police, and Pharisees who are fixated on skirt or sleeve length. Anyone who understands that Jesus looks on the heart, not the outward appearance, should have no difficulty exchanging their religious rules for a simpler dress code that can be written down with one word: Modesty.

Why do loving pastors so often give legalists a pass? Has political correctness caused mild mannered preachers to lose the stomach for war? Politeness and compromise with mean religion never leads to peace. The legalistic spirits which energize mean religion killed Jesus and Paul; and they did it without dirtying their religious hands. They incited others to do their dirty work. These same spirits are at work in the church today. Left unchallenged, they will annihilate those who have forgotten how to "fight the good fight of faith."

We are not fighting against flesh and blood. Our controversy against religious spirits is a dreadful war with demonic forces of darkness that are intent on dragging their victims into a prison of horrible bondage. You cannot make a truce with such forces. Victory in this war can only be won by true soldiers of the cross who are willing to pay a price to deliver souls in bondage. True soldiers of the cross long for peace – but not the false peace of the compromisers. They will press the battle until the true liberty purchased by blood at Calvary is won.

These seasoned veterans of the cross know from past wounds and painful experience that there can be only one kind of peace with the malign spirits of legalism and bondage: the kind that comes when the battle is over, the dust settles, and all the enemies lay motionless at your feet. It is a costly peace bought with the blood of Christian soldiers who love the bound enough to fight the evil that binds them. Though weary from many battles, they will stand and fight until they breathe the intoxicating air of total victory.

Such soldiers are rare in this age of comfort and compromise, but some are yet among us. They are determined men and women who love authentic Christianity which liberates and hate legalistic religion which binds. They are honorable, politically incorrect men and women who refuse to *"give place to the devil"* (Ephesians 4:27).

They are not for sale. Their love for the Lamb, and those for whom He died, is stronger than their love for life. They are tough enough to endure rejection and secure enough to sacrifice popularity. They refuse to congregate with the politically correct who remain silent while legalistic devils drag new believers into religious bondage. They lift their voices knowing that they will be criticized, condemned, slandered and misrepresented by angry legalists. They willingly fight the evil others choose to ignore, or fail to see. And they fight with the understanding that even many of those for whom they fight will join those who condemn them. They fight because Jesus fought. In the fight against legalism, they become hardened soldiers; but just beneath the toughness you will find hearts that are tender toward the victims of the mean religion they confront.

With discernment and love, they take the battle to the gates of hell and fight what others fail to recognize as the enemy. In faithful duty on the field of battle, they become honorable soldiers who dutifully devote their lives to fight an evil others can't comprehend. Believing in the power of the blood of Jesus, and loving the liberty bought with blood, they resist the evil of religion which returns the redeemed to former bondage. May their numbers grow.

The Church must remember that we are an army at war with a world system ruled by Satan, *"the prince of the power of the air"* (Ephesians 2:2). This world is a battleground, though many act as if it were a playground. Satan's rule extends to the religious systems – legalistic and liberal – which have compromised with the world system. When we identify the spiritual enemies driving these systems, and begin to fight them with weapons of war which are not carnal, we will see souls delivered from bondage.

Even some of the leaders of legalistic religion will repent. Saul, a legalistic Pharisee who was the fiercest persecutor of Christians on the planet, was won by love. He never forgot the love and forgiveness of Stephen who asked God to forgive the angry Pharisees while they were in the very act of stoning him: *"And cast him out of the city, and stoned him: and the witnesses laid down their clothes at a young man's feet, whose name was Saul. And they stoned Stephen, calling upon God, and saying,*

Lord Jesus, receive my spirit. And he kneeled down, and cried with a loud voice, Lord, lay not this sin to their charge. And when he had said this, he fell asleep (Acts 7:58-60).

True soldiers of the cross will welcome the repentant because beneath the toughness beats a tender heart. God grant that those who fight the evil others have not yet seen or understood may be like Joseph. Let us remember his heart, and the words he spoke to the brothers who betrayed him and caused him years of horrible pain and agony. When he found himself in a place of power and his betrayers were bowing at his feet, he pronounced forgiveness on them and, with love and magnanimity, spoke these words: *"And Joseph said unto them, Fear not: for am I in the place of God? But as for you, ye thought evil against me; but God meant it unto good, to bring to pass, as it is this day, to save much people alive. Now therefore fear ye not: I will nourish you, and your little ones..."* (Genesis 50:19-21).

The true soldiers of the cross will prevail over mean religion, and over all the forces of evil that resist the rule of the Lamb who loved us and washed us from our sins in His own blood. Though we may be called mean-spirited by those who somewhere on the journey lost the stomach for war, may we continue the fight with love in our hearts and be always ready to embrace the repentant. Let us continue the fight knowing that one day, on a battlefield where all the enemies of the glorious gospel will be silenced, we will lift our voices and proclaim to the glory of the great Captain of our Salvation, *"And they overcame him by the blood of the Lamb and by the word of their testimony; and they loved not their lives unto the death"* (Revelation 12:11).

Chapter One

Small-Brained Religion

Jesus established a kingdom that opened the door of heaven to people on earth. He populated the kingdom with a redeemed family, bound together by loving relationships. That family is His Church: A body of believers joined together by the Holy Spirit. Man has messed it up by building many different kingdoms under the banner of religion. Many of these earthly kingdoms have become dead religious organizations held together and governed by man-made doctrines and traditions, rules and rituals. The kingdom Jesus established is a living organism bound together by covenant love experienced in spiritual relationships. Religion is the shadow; relationship is the substance. Religion is a dead human system which does not contain the power of reproduction. Christianity – authentic Christianity – is a living organism with the power to reproduce the life of Jesus.

The following pages are a rather irreverent exposé of just one sectarian segment of the mess man created: Religious legalism - small-brained religion which "dulls the mind and chills the heart" (A.W.Tozer). Before proceeding further, let me issue a warning to laughing liberals who might find this humorous reading: Don't laugh too loudly. Your day will come. Modern liberals have often swung so far to the other side of the pendulum that they no longer have convictions about anything. Liberalism, on the surface, may not seem as messed up as legalism but it is actually quite dangerous. It has carried grace to the point of lawlessness. The laws liberals think grace did away with are written on our hearts. We have been freed from the tyranny of external religion by a loving God who desires to have fellowship with us but He didn't leave His moral law outside the door when He walked into our hearts. There is another side of grace which desperately needs to be re-discovered." Paul wrote about it in Titus 2:11-12: *"For the grace of God that brings salvation has appeared to all: teaching us that, denying ungodliness and worldly lusts, we should live soberly, righteously, and godly, in this present world."*

But that is the subject of a later book; our subject here is legalism. My purpose is not only to reveal why Jesus hated it, but to help its prisoners escape from it. I know from personal experience that there is hope, even for the worst kind of legalist, if he truly wants to be enlightened. Jesus hates legalistic religion. He operates outside its foreboding walls and enters it only to confront its taskmasters and deliver its captives. When His mission on earth is complete, there will be no religion remaining. There will be one King and one Kingdom: A

Kingdom built on relationship and ruled by righteous love, not the rules of religion.

Can love hate? Is that an oxymoron? I don't think so. Hate can't love, but love can hate. In the modern world of polite seeker-sensitive Christianity, love has lost all its convictions. It embraces everything and won't stand against anything. It has forgotten how to say "sin." But real love has the power to confront evil in the world or in the church. God is love and the Bible lists several things He hates in Proverbs 6:16-19. Pride heads the list and legalism is a manifestation of pride. The disdain of Jesus for the legalistic system of man-made doctrines, rules, and rituals practiced by the Pharisees leaves no doubt: Love hates legalism. Religious legalism is an insidious evil which frustrates and discourages those oppressed by it. It robs people of the peace and joy of salvation. Many Christian leaders realize it is wicked and oppressive, yet they allow it to operate in their churches. Why?

Why does a loving pastor allow something that discourages and frustrates new believers to operate unchallenged? Why do we tolerate something that causes children who love Jesus to grow up to be teenagers who run from our churches? Are we blind to the pervasive influence of legalism? Are we confused by it, or conflicted because of it? Are mild-mannered pastors afraid to confront it?

Some leave it alone because they confuse it with holiness. But there is nothing holy about legalism. Legalism produces death; holiness produces life. Jesus hated legalism and fought it throughout the course of His ministry. He fought it because he saw it for what it is: Mean narrow-minded religion. The difference between religious legalism and holiness born of the Spirit is easily perceived: Legalism is an external thing that clothes itself with man-made rules and regulations; holiness is a quality of inward beauty that flows from a heart governed by love. Legalism burdens and binds; holiness lifts and liberates. Love goes deeper than external rules and regulations and communes with holy law written internally on a redeemed heart. Legalism controls by fear; perfect love casts out fear. Legalism condemns; love frees from condemnation (Romans 8:1-2).

Legalism lays burdens too heavy to bear on new Christians and leaves them frustrated and discouraged. It causes well-meaning parents to be overly strict with their children, hoping to make them behave like good little Christians. Legalism embarrasses Christian youth by forcing them to conform to codes of dress and conduct that invite rejection. It won't allow them to participate in wholesome activities with their peers. It won't allow girls to play on the volleyball, basketball, or track teams because they would have to wear shorts.

The fruit of legalism should lead one to conclude that it is an insidious evil that needs to be exposed and confronted by every loving leader interested in protecting the people in his care. Many clearly see it as sin but they tolerate it because it just doesn't seem as bad as adultery, stealing, and other sins they would go after. Rare is the pastor within such systems who is willing to hit it head on – even when he begins to see it for what it is. And there are very few outside the small world of mean, legalistic religion, who even bother to address it. A lot of leaders have forgotten how to say the word "sin." They are certainly not going to confront what they won't even say. The modern model of pastor, which is often sugar coated with niceness, doesn't look much like earlier models. The modern pastor often appears to be more interested in being nice and popular, than in acting like a real shepherd charged with not only feeding, but protecting the sheep.

Legalism is mean. It mocks nice Christianity. It plays with polite preachers who traded their convictions for compromise. Jesus and the Apostles were different. They were not nice to legalists and they didn't set out to win a popularity contest. They met legalism with conviction and force that sent it stuttering away. The soft-spoken, nice-guy pastor would not approve of the way Jesus and Paul operated. Their leadership style would wreck his cozy congregation in one meeting. They were not mild-mannered motivational speakers who scratched itching ears. They were strong preachers who declared the whole counsel of God in the power of the Spirit. They knew how to say "sin" and deep conviction often followed their preaching.

I am not advocating a return to old time religion that was "good enough for Ma and Pa," but I am suggesting that it would be difficult to improve on the model exemplified by Jesus and the Apostles. Their styles and methods are still relevant and culture-current because they followed the Bible pattern of leadership, and the Bible is ageless. It transcends culture. Its message is still as revolutionary as it was in the first century. In some nations, where the Bible model is still in vogue, leaders preach the gospel with fire fueled by the fullness of the Spirit and see results not unlike those of the New Testament Church. In America, where pastors are often more interested in new programs than in power and a fresh baptism of the Holy Spirit and fire, we don't see the same results. Honest leaders cut through all the hype and admit that, in relation to the growth of the population, the church in America is losing ground. And sadly, our greatest loss is our youth who are running from powerless churches.

Our nation is crying for preachers like those of the New Testament, preachers who are willing to address both sides of the pendulum – mean legalism and polite liberalism. America needs preachers who know how to preach the truth in love, and who understand that love can be firm, even violent, with its enemies. And legalism is an enemy of love. That is why the most loving Person who ever set foot on this planet hated legalism with holy passion. He hated it because it deeply hurt the objects of His love. We should hate it, too. Legalism limits the release of the Spirit's power. Our youth know the difference between fleshly displays of emotion and the true moving of the Holy Spirit – and they are not willing to play religious games.

Youth are not so easily fooled by false signs and wonders that the deluded call miracles. Our youth are not running from Christianity. They are leaving a cold religion that "chills the heart." They are crying for a true demonstration of the real Holy Spirit. We don't need more programs; we need power. Nothing else will even get the attention of this younger generation. They live behind a virtual force-field in a cyber space world that can only be penetrated by power: The same power that came like a mighty rushing wind, with tongues of fire, into an Upper Room in Jerusalem over 2000 years ago. We need leaders who will pay the price for exposing legalistic religion and return to the real Pentecostal Christianity of the first century: A Christianity infused with power which produced 3,000 converts with its first sermon. We need "real religion" which will rock our modern world the way New Testament Christianity rocked the ancient Roman Empire.

Legalism is small-brained Christianity which drives multitudes of Christian youth out of the church into the world's waiting arms. Young children love Jesus but as they grow older they often become bored with church. They long for the day when they will be old enough to walk away from the bondage and boredom. When that day comes many cast off restraint, rebel and go wild. Legalistic pastors and bewildered parents ask what happened to the little darlings who used to love Jesus. They shake their heads and wonder what is wrong with this younger generation. They refuse to face the truth: These youth are not rejecting Jesus; they are rejecting a legalistic misrepresentation of Him.

Chapter Two

The Holy Ghost Made Me Do It

I knew little about religion as a child. I learned that it could be both weird and mean when I was nine years old and went to church for the first time. A boy in my class at school invited me to visit the little Pentecostal holiness church his family attended, and I went to a midweek meeting. I was like a lamb led to the slaughter. I had not a clue what I was about to experience. The following well-remembered account is so bizarre, some of you will swear I am being "evangelastic," but it is true. (It is a bit embellished, but it actually happened to me). I am still traumatized by the memory fifty-five years later.

The air was filled with singing often interrupted by shouting. In the middle of what was called a special song, the pastor jumped from the platform and started running around the church shouting, "Holy Ghost! Holy Ghost!" After a couple of laps, even the old ladies started running, or walking as fast as they could, in the line behind the pastor. After a while, I was running with them. I was afraid not to. When I realized that I was the only person still in my seat, I jumped up and got going. I ran and ran, but I didn't say "Holy Ghost! Holy Ghost!"

I was relieved when everybody sat down but the relief was short- lived. You may not believe this. You might think I am just rehearsing an old episode of "The Twilight Zone," but seconds after sitting back down, a skinny, wild-eyed man flew past me shouting "Hallelujah" and jumping from pew to pew. I later learned you had to be anointed or "in the Spirit" to do that. This guy must have been super-anointed because he didn't fall until he hit the last pew. I think he would have made it all the way but he got distracted by a rather large lady making squealing noises as she jumped up and down by the back door. I later learned that she was "dancing in the Spirit."

It all went downhill after that. My nine year old, first-time-in-church, brain was suffering sensory overload. Runners, pew jumpers, and big "dancing" ladies with top-knots: It was too much. But the worst was yet to come. Soon, everybody went to the altar – except me. Strange things were going on up there. I just wanted to go home but that wasn't happening. One of the older ladies in a long dress and hair in a top-knot saw me sitting back there all by myself and came to rescue me. She took me by the hand and "helped" me to the altar. I immediately became the center of attention. The entire group surrounded me and several took turns laying hands on me.

It was a bad deal. I got a Holy Ghost rubdown that left my hair all messed up. Excited prayer warriors pounced on me and prayed over me in a foreign language. They kept saying "let go or just release it." I was really confused. Several people were at the same time shouting things like "Glory," "Jesus" and "Hallelujah." Others were saying things that sounded something like "Ba ba ba and sha la la," or "Kum ba yah." I was traumatized. Remember, this was the first time I had ever attended church.

I love and reverence the precious Holy Spirit. I cringe even rehearsing a story like this. I don't understand how people, who appear to be clothed and in their right minds, can act in such a manner and then call it the moving of the Holy Ghost. The real Holy Ghost does not operate in an atmosphere of fleshly outbursts and religious confusion. Something was moving in that meeting but it was not the precious Spirit of God. It was flesh and emotion worked up by religious people striving to make something happen themselves. It is sad that so many churches, when they don't "feel" the moving of the Spirit, try to stir something up in the flesh. They become people driven by a desire to experience emotional release in every meeting. Like drug addicts who need a regular "fix," they become "meeting junkies" who don't feel like they have had church unless some crazy stuff has taken place.

I have seen crazier things than I saw in that meeting as a nine year old. Through the course of forty years in ministry, I have observed preachers manipulate crowds all over the world. I have seen them try one thing after another until some "willing to be manipulated" person, or a few of them, jumps in the water. Others always join them and before long the "Holy Ghost" blowout is on. We should be grieved that preachers are willing to manipulate flesh and emotion and call it the moving of the Spirit. We should be ashamed that so few people in such churches have the spiritual discernment to know the difference between manipulated flesh and the true moving of the Spirit.

In some churches, anything goes. I have watched people try to teach an innocent "victim" at an altar to speak in tongues. I have watched people take hold of someone's jaws and move them up and down, trying to get them to let loose in other tongues. I have watched preachers try to get through a poorly prepared sermon while an "intercessor" who couldn't hold it back, babbled loudly in tongues and shouted "Hallelujah, Jesus" intermittently through the entire sermon. I have tried to talk to such people, but I always here basically the same thing from them that I here from those who interrupt a sermon with a message in tongues or a prophetic utterance: "When the Holy Ghost moves on me I can't hold it back," or, "I can't control it."

I have referred many of these "spiritual" people to 1 Corinthians 14:32: *"And the spirits of the prophets are subject to the prophets."* They usually look at me like I am from another planet and pity me because I just don't get it. I go on to tell them that, *"God is not the author of confusion, but of peace (order), as in all the churches of the saints,"* and that Paul instructed, *"Let all things be done decently and in order" (1 Corinthians 14:40).*

When they continue to stare at me like I am speaking a foreign language, I go on to explain that it is not in order to distract or disturb people around you who are trying to enter into worship, or actually trying to hear what the preacher is saying. That seldom helps either, so I go on to explain that the Holy Spirit doesn't interrupt Himself. It stands to reason that if the anointing is on the worship leaders, it must not be on those who are babbling so loudly in "tongues" that those around them are so distracted they can't worship. It stands to reason that if the preacher is anointed, it must not be the Holy Spirit who interrupts him mid-sentence with a message in tongues or a prophetic utterance. Common sense alone should cause such people to wait for a pause in the service and speak at an appropriate moment.

Not everyone who behaves this way has an unruly, religious spirit. Sometimes it is simply learned behavior. New Christians are all eyes and ears. Most want to learn. They come into meetings and observe what goes on. They develop an idea of what is acceptable behavior by watching those thought to be spiritual. If the leaders allow it and, especially, if they encourage it, new believers will soon be imitating the behavior of those whom they assume are spiritual. We need to pray for the leader who knows better but allows this process to be repeated, over and over again, because he doesn't want to make waves or upset some unruly devil. By his tolerance and apathy, he is allowing impressionable new believers to be contaminated by rude religious spirits.

These behaviors are an affront to the order for which Paul contended in I Corinthians 14. I don't allow them in churches or meetings where I have leadership responsibility. I have a firm conviction that the Spirit leads but He doesn't drive. It is ludicrous to excuse unruly or disorderly behavior by saying, "I couldn't help it. The Holy Ghost moved on me and I couldn't hold it back." The truth is you can hold it back and you can wait for an opportune moment, perhaps a pause in the service, and then allow the Holy Spirit to lead you to move in one of the gifts of the Spirit. I don't want to work anything up in the flesh. If the Spirit moves, I want it to be because we waited and listened with sensitivity for His leading.

It takes nothing away from the moving of the Spirit to establish and teach guidelines for worship in our meetings, but we have been accused of controlling or restricting the moving of the Spirit for doing so. The truth is we are restricting the moving of the "flesh" in order to facilitate an atmosphere in which the Spirit is free to move – the way He wants to – "decently and in order." We don't let unruly people, who often travel in the company of religious spirits, get away with the excuse, "The Holy Ghost made me do it."

If you allow such people to "do their thing" in your meetings, there will always be chaos and a lack of order. People whose brains are firing on all cylinders will often saturate the atmosphere with their absence after such meetings and you will eventually be left with only the unruly and those who entertain stubborn religious spirits. It is for these reasons, and for such people, that we establish guidelines like the few which follow:

1) The Bible is the inspired, infallible Word of God. It is the final authority, the rule, for all our faith and practice.

2) The Word and the Spirit are always in perfect agreement; they never contradict one other.

3) The Holy Spirit never interrupts Himself.

I got home late after that Wednesday night meeting at the legalistic church in northern California – too late for a nine year old kid who had to go to school the next day. I tried to explain it all to my parents but it was a little difficult. The next day my teacher kept asking me if I was OK. She let me lay my head on my desk and take a nap after I told her I didn't go to bed until almost midnight. I was glad she didn't ask why.

A week later my religious friend invited me to another service. I let all the pent up effects of trauma from the previous meeting loose without warning. I didn't say "Thanks, but no." I just hit him in the nose so hard that blood splattered all over his white shirt and he ran away crying. After that, I learned that some brands of religion are mean wherever you encounter them – in or out of church. My little religious friend had two older, church-going cousins. I had to fight them at school the next day. They would have probably beaten me down but when my new cowboy hat got messed up in the dirt I got angry. They found out that something in me was meaner than their religion.

I felt better until my teacher introduced me to the "board of education." The religious cousins didn't get the privilege of meeting the "board". It seems that the wielder of the "board" concluded that I had to be the culprit in this altercation. The religious cousins were thought to be good little Christians. Everyone knew I was a pure blooded heathen. I didn't have a chance. I don't know if my teacher was religious, but she was definitely mean. This whole deal started with an invitation to a meeting. I had my fill of church and Christians at the ripe old age of nine.

Chapter Three

Will The Real Holy Ghost Please Stand Up?

My family relocated shortly after the fight at school. We moved from the redwood forests of northern California to the asphalt jungles of north St. Louis. It was a tough adjustment. It didn't escape my attention that the whole ordeal seemed somehow connected to the downward spiral that began when I attended church for the first time in my life.

We moved into a second story apartment above my Aunt Clara. I might have never darkened the doors of a church again, if not for her prayer and persistence. She seemed sort of nice but I was a little skeptical because she was one of those church people. She had it bad. She went twice on Sunday and every Wednesday. She was a Baptist and over time was successful in convincing me that the Baptists were nicer than the pew jumping legalists I had been exposed to. But what really moved me to go to church with her one Sunday in March of 1959 was the church ball team. All you had to do was attend Sunday school three times a month to meet the requirements to play on the team. You didn't even have to go to the altar, if you didn't want to.

I thank God for the Baptists. My Sunday school teacher was boring but the pastor was great. He helped me understand that God loved me and that He would become my heavenly Father, if I would just receive His Son Jesus. I went to the altar without help and no one pounced on me. The big pastor just took my hand and led me in a prayer. This was definitely nicer religion. He patted me on the head but it didn't even mess up my hair.

Thanks to a Baptist softball league and an aunt who wasn't a religious nutcase (She wore her hair bun-style but she didn't jump up and down and squeal like a baby pig) my home life got a lot better. My whole family came to the meeting when I was baptized. They went forward and prayed to receive Jesus and later joined the church. We began attending together - twice on Sunday and every Wednesday.

Some Pentecostals who lived next door had been silent up to that point but, upon discovering we were attending church, they suddenly became interested in us. They tried to dissuade us from attending St. Louis Park Baptist Church and come with them to some kind of tabernacle where the "power was flowing." They said the Baptists didn't know anything about that. I got scared when my dad seemed interested. I didn't know that there were different kinds of Pentecostals. I figured they were all like the ones I encountered in California. It scared me to see my dad getting interested in what they had to say.

They told us that the Baptists didn't have the Holy Ghost and that we needed the "fullness." I was more interested in playing ball than in learning about the "fullness." I was just a kid but I had more experience with the Holy Ghost than the other members of the family. I told our Pentecostal neighbors that the Baptists did have a Holy Ghost and that He was not as mean as the one I met in California. I was a little nervous that my parents might want to visit their church but when I reminded them about all the trouble my last experience with the Pentecostals had brought on the family, they decided to remain Baptists. In those days, I normally just lay in bed and prayed, "Now I lay me down to sleep. I pray the Lord my soul to keep. And if I should die before I wake, I pray the Lord my soul to take. Amen." But that night I got down on my knees and did some serious praying. I wanted to play ball with the Baptists, not get lessons in linguistics from the Pentecostals.

My usual little prayer just didn't seem sufficient. I wanted to be delivered from a horrible repeat of history. I had nightmares that night about bloody noses, vindictive religious cousins and mad principals. I saw pew jumpers and dancing ladies wearing top-knots. I was relieved to wake up to the smell of bacon cooking and to learn at breakfast that we were still

Baptists. My Sunday school teacher even seemed more interesting that morning. The thought of another excursion into the world of mean religion changed my opinion of him.

My interest in church soon grew beyond the ball team. I actually enjoyed it and my family got a lot closer for a few years. But trouble came unexpectedly and my parents separated. I grew bitter and when I turned fourteen I made the worst decision of my life: I left the church and turned my back on Jesus – a decision that led to years of rebellion, drunkenness and drugs. But God had mercy on me and I survived. Several years later a Baptist preacher was sitting at my kitchen table telling me that God still loved me. I was mad and everybody who had partied with me the night before knew it. Nobody would tell me who let him in. After being up all night I didn't care to talk to a preacher. I told him that his church was full of hypocrites and that half of them spent an inordinate amount of time gossiping about me. That didn't discourage or slow him down, so I turned up the heat. I told him that he could take his church and all the hypocrites in it and go straight to "you know where."

Even that didn't faze him. This poor Baptist pastor, so pitied by those who said he didn't have the Holy Ghost, had more love for lost souls than the whole miserable lot of legalists I had encountered in my short time on the planet. He was the real deal. He looked straight into my blurry, bloodshot eyes and said, "Say whatever you want to, I still love you and Jesus still loves you."

I knew I had to get this guy out the door. So, one more time, I gave him the hypocrites' spiel. He still didn't get mad. He didn't get offended and storm out of my house. He didn't even defend his church. He simply smiled and said, "You are right. There are hypocrites in my church and they are going to hell. The bad news is that you are going to be with them unless you repent and get right with Jesus."

That messed me up. I would rather be in hell with some of the people I had been in jail with than with some of the hypocrites at his church. I never forgot that pastor. A few months later I repented (during an acid trip) and gave my life to Jesus. My first thought was that I wanted to go to his church. They were nice to me even though I had long hair and a beard. I thought I had found a church that wasn't afflicted with mean religion.

About a month after beginning again with the Baptists, I met a group of Pentecostals who seemed to have their heads screwed on straighter than the ones in California. They didn't jump pews or drag nine year olds to the altar and scare the devil out of them. They didn't even have dancing, top-knotted ladies. They didn't pressure me and didn't tell me I was not saved because I had not yet spoken in other tongues.

But when I got interested in the power of the Spirit, things got confusing again. Some of the Baptists started warning me to stay away from my new Pentecostal friends. When I didn't heed their advice, some sort of latent meanness began coming to the surface. I tried to explain that these Pentecostals were different. They showed me love and shared scriptures on the baptism of the Holy Spirit. They didn't get pushy or belligerent but, I must admit, it was a bit scary because I still had a few brain cells left which had recorded images and memories of my experience as a nine year old. I was torn and didn't know who was right.

As time passed, I saw that my new friends truly were different. They seemed to have a level of excitement and joy that was beyond anything I had experienced at that time. They didn't pressure me to get a haircut or shave. They didn't seem to mind that I wore jeans and T-shirts to their meetings. No one ever said a word about my appearance.

There was something about them that intrigued me and their love finally won me over. I began studying and seeking the fullness of the Spirit. I prayed and prayed. I became so hungry and thirsty for the baptism of the Spirit that I often woke up and prayed through the night.

I was still a little traumatized at the thought of going to an altar and being pounced on by the nutcases who were always on the hunt for people like me, but the trauma was trumped by the desire for what I read about in the book of Acts. I was still confused because I kept hearing one thing from my Baptist friends – several of whom had shown me a lot of love – and another thing from my new Pentecostal friends. I finally decided not to listen to either group.

So, I just kept praying alone, determined to figure this thing out for myself without listening to the Baptists or the Pentecostals. I studied and studied and often prayed late into the night. I wanted everything God had for me, but I didn't want to become "weird" like the Pentecostals I had encountered at the little church in California. After several months, I became convinced through my own study of the Bible that I needed the baptism of the Holy Ghost. Driving home late one night, I prayed this simple prayer: "God, Peter had it. Paul had it. I don't see why I shouldn't have it. Lord, I ask you to baptize me in the Holy Spirit right now."

A volcano erupted from deep within (It doesn't have to happen that way, but it did for me). I started speaking in other tongues and continued doing so all the way home. I was driving my 56 Chevrolet panel truck which people used to follow to parties. Following it after my conversion would usually lead you to church or somewhere to give out tracts and witness. That old party bus had attracted a lot of attention lately. The morning after I gave my life to Jesus, I painted it. On the front and back I painted in huge letters, "JESUS SAVES." On the passenger side I painted in bigger letters with a can of white spray paint, "JESUS IS COMING." On the driver's side, which had parked against a tree on the way home from a party one morning, I painted, "LIFE A WRECK? TRY JESUS." That is where I got the Baptism: In my converted panel truck, all alone with Jesus. People told me it couldn't happen that way, but it did. I was still talking in tongues when I walked into my little cabin and continued until about three in the morning.

Talking in tongues was just part of the package. I received what Jesus promised: Power to witness. I became more excited about witnessing on the streets and door to door. The Holy Spirit was flowing through me, working with me, helping me to reach the lost. I felt a deeper sense of God's presence and experienced new freedom in worship. I took Paul's advice and began "*singing in the Spirit and with the understanding also*") 1

Corinthians 14:15). I listened to Jude and started *"building myself up in faith, praying in the Holy Ghost"* (Jude 20).

Chapter Four

The Devil Made Him Do It

A deeper sense of purpose filled my life. The Bible seemed more alive to me. I witnessed to the lost everywhere I went with greater confidence and power. Was this what the believers in the Upper Room had experienced? I couldn't wait to go to church and tell my Baptist friends that the baptism in the Holy Spirit was real and that it didn't end with the Apostles. I testified of my experience but they did not share my excitement. In fact, they tried to convince me that I had been deceived. That is when I met another kind of mean.

These loving people didn't feel comfortable around "tongue talkers" – even when they weren't talking in tongues. They were convinced it was the devil who made me do it and that speaking in other tongues ended in the first century. When I insisted that it didn't, some got even meaner. A lot of phones were on party lines in those days and the whole neighborhood quickly learned that I had lost my mind. Everybody in the sub-division who wasn't calling somebody else to tell them what the ex-hippie was doing now, was just listening in on other peoples' conversations. Several members of the church kept things stirred up until the deacons felt it necessary to have a special business meeting; I was the first item on the agenda. The crowd was a record breaker. The atmosphere was charged and I soon learned why. The head deacon called the business meeting to order and a motion was made and seconded to hold a vote on whether or not to allow me to continue attending the church. I got "the left foot of fellowship." They voted me out of the church.

That was my first lesson in church politics. Those who wanted me to stay and continue in youth ministry outnumbered those who wanted me to leave. They liked having so many new youth in the church and felt that God was moving and setting the stage for revival. They were willing to reach out in love to my "improperly groomed" friends and give God time to work. That didn't matter. The only votes that counted were those of the official members. That experience still serves to remind me how quickly even some nice people can become very mean when you don't play by their rules and embrace their cherished doctrines.

I was a new Christian and didn't understand why people were so upset that I had experienced what the believers in the book of Acts had experienced. I left that church wondering if I would ever figure it out. I didn't ask anyone to leave with me but seventy-five youth and young adults followed me out. The official members let it be known that they would rather have a smaller congregation than a church filled with people like me.

My "fame" continued to grow. The loose-lipped gossips in the church talked about me even more the next week. My phone just kept ringing. Some of the calls were from pastors who had scheduled me for a meeting. Some had already advertised that I would be with them to give a testimony of deliverance and salvation. A lot of people loved to hear the stories of deliverance, but I guess they lost interest when the Holy Ghost got involved. I was told by numerous pastors and church members that they got all the Holy Ghost they needed when they were baptized by immersion in the name of the Father, Son, and Holy Ghost. They were convinced that talking in tongues went out with the Apostles and, therefore, something other than the Holy Ghost was talking through me.

I had my fill of church politics and gossip but I still loved Jesus. Many of those who left when I did asked me to start holding meetings. That wasn't in my plans. I wanted to go to Bible school somewhere. But after a month of praying without success for the Lord to send another leader, I rented a store front building on Highway 30 in House Springs, Missouri and the word spread like wildfire. Young people throughout the area started coming to Friday and Saturday night meetings. There was a mixture of Baptists, Methodists, Lutherans, Pentecostals, and heathens. We started bringing in Christian bands and soon we had two or three hundred young people attending each night. A big part of the crowd was different every week. I was experiencing a revival before I even knew what revival was. I had no idea what to do so I just prayed a lot.

Then something happened that caused the whole religious community to explode. One Saturday night the Holy Spirit fell on a group of youth who had come from First Baptist Church in House Springs. They began to spontaneously speak in other tongues. I had not touched one of them but it didn't help explaining that to their pastor and parents. I got all the blame for what God had done!

The youth went to church the following night and gave testimonies of their experience. The church should have been excited that these youth, who normally sat in the back, talked and cut up during the service, were now participating - but they weren't. They were mad. There was hot water in House Springs and I was swimming in it.

Following that incident, I began receiving calls and personal visits from pastors and more prominent members of the association. In the recent past, they had been excited about the positive influence I was having on youth. They had arranged meetings at school assemblies, civic clubs and churches. Some even supported me financially. But my relationship with them changed overnight. Our conversations were different now. I think they were all reading from the same script. After failing to convince me to deny my "unscriptural experience," they warned me that the devil could make me talk in tongues. I told them I had been asking God, not the devil, for the experience and that I didn't believe God would let the devil give me something bad when I was asking Him for something good. I told them that my position was supported by numerous scriptures like Luke 11:13, "If *ye then, being evil, know how to give good gifts unto your children: how much more shall your heavenly Father give the Holy Spirit to them that ask him?*" That seemed to upset them more. The more verses I gave them, the more unpleasant the conversations became.

Even bigger guns came after me when the calls and visits didn't return me to sanity. All the doors that had been open to me were slammed and locked tight. I was blacklisted. I learned from a pastor, who jumped at opportunities to tell people what he had been told not to repeat, that I had been the main topic of discussion at the latest county association meetings. I think I even got attention at the state level. An influential pastor informed the association that I had to be stopped. He convinced his fellow pastors that I was like a spiritual "Pied Piper" with some kind of strange power over youth.

Things were really stirred up but it wasn't because of me. It was because the precious Holy Spirit moved on a group of young people. Remember, I didn't touch one of them. The Spirit of God stirred their hearts and they got excited about serving Jesus. Everyone else should have been excited, too. But rigid doctrinal positions kept them from being open minded. The dramatic change in the lives of many of the youth was clearly evident but that didn't matter.

One mother said, "I would rather see my children running around smoking pot than to have them in those meetings speaking in other tongues." She got her wish. When she refused to allow them to attend the Friday and Saturday night meetings they started hanging out with their old friends and going to parties. The world was waiting for them with open arms.

It is unsettling to suddenly become aware of the sort of things that can be hiding behind a nice religious smile. I felt discouraged but I knew the Bible says we should rejoice under such circumstances. I realized that there are worse things than having people speak evil against you falsely. The worst insult the devil can pay you is to ignore you. I had met mean religion earlier. This was mean religion wearing another mask; it was mean in a different way. It was not like the legalism I had previously encountered, but they must have been second cousins. I realized that they were different expressions of the same thing: a religious spirit that was determined to discourage and hinder me. One wanted to load me down with legalism. The other wanted to deprive me of the power promised by Jesus to the Apostles and to all who would believe what they preached. *"But you shall receive power, after the Holy Ghost is come upon you: and ye shall be witnesses unto me...." "For the promise is unto you, and to your children, and to all that are afar off, even as many as the Lord our God shall call (Acts 1:8 and 2:39).*

People I thought were friends suddenly turned on me because I embraced a doctrine they didn't believe. But I still love and appreciate the Baptists. They helped me understand God's love as a child, after legalistic Pentecostals had scared me. I went to St. Louis Park Baptist Church for one reason - to play on a ball team. But God had something else in mind. I had a head-on collision with the love that caused Jesus to lay down his life for me. The pastor loved lost souls and he was great at communicating the Gospel to children. Week after week, I heard sermons of God's love and forgiveness in an atmosphere where you could actually hear the message. He didn't run around the church for twenty minutes saying nothing except "Holy

Ghost! Holy Ghost!" He presented the glorious Gospel clearly and gave intelligent altar calls. I thank God for the Baptists. Without them, I may never have started reading the Bible again - and reading the Bible is what convinced me that there was a real Holy Ghost Who was different from the one the legalists claimed to have.

In over forty years of ministry, I have never jumped pews nor ran around a church saying nothing but "Holy Ghost! Holy Ghost!" By God's grace, I have been spared a lot of the sort of weirdness that causes so many to reject the Pentecostal message. But I have enjoyed wonderful communion with the precious Holy Spirit. He has been my Comforter and Friend. He has guided, instructed and helped me. He has made Jesus more real to me. He has moved my heart with compassion for the lost and the hurting. He has anointed me to preach the Gospel in power throughout the world. I love Him. I need Him. I daily depend on Him. I can't imagine life without Him. To those who have been confused or discouraged by mean religion, I plead, "Give the real Holy Ghost a chance. Seek Him until you find Him. You will not be disappointed."

Chapter Five

Jesus Was Not Nice to the Legalists

Religious legalism is a wicked thing. It warps people. It traumatizes nine year old heathens. It acts like it loves you, but turns on you the moment you refuse to bow to it. Enlightened Christians should confront and rebuke it, not tolerate it. Jesus confronted the Pharisees. Paul took the Judaizers (converted Pharisees) to task. Both boldly confronted legalists and warned others to avoid their poison. They were not passive. They challenged anything that hindered, frustrated, or perverted the grace of God.

Jesus hated legalism with holy passion. He exposed its evils at every opportunity. He went so far as to deliberately provoke the Pharisees. Why? Legalists prefer to operate in the dark. Jesus knew their nature, so He forced them to come out of the shadows. He provoked them to expose them. He knew they were snakes, but others didn't. Jesus forced them to step out from behind phony faces of respectable religion so others could see what they were. Jesus saw behind every mask they wore. They hated Him because He recognized and exposed their hypocrisy.

Does it shock you to think that the "gentle" Jesus would deliberately provoke someone? He did. How? In many ways: By breaking their rules, by hanging out with sinners, by sitting down and conversing with an adulterous woman at a well, by bringing a former demon possessed woman into His inner circle. How did He provoke them? By calling them fools, snakes, hypocrites, white-washed tombs, etc. One must wonder if the nice, non-combative Christianity of our day could handle this Jesus. (If you still need help seeing this side of the "gentle" Jesus, read passages like Matthew 15:1-14 and all of chapter 23, or Luke 11: 37-52).

"Ye hypocrites, well did Esaias prophesy of you, saying, this people draweth nigh to me with their mouth, and honoreth me with their lips, but their heart is far from me. But in vain they do worship me, teaching for doctrines the commandments of men" (Matthew 15: 7-9).

"But all their works they do to be seen of men: But woe unto you, scribes and Pharisees, hypocrites! For ye shut up the kingdom of heaven against men: for ye neither go in yourselves, neither suffer ye them that are entering to go in... Ye blind guides which strain at a gnat, and swallow a camel...Woe unto you, scribes, Pharisees, and hypocrites! For ye make clean the outside of the cup but within they are full of extortion and

excess...Woe unto you scribes, Pharisees, hypocrites! For ye are like whited sepulchers, which indeed appear beautiful outward, but are within full of dead men's bones, and of all uncleanness...Ye serpents, ye generation of vipers, how can ye escape the damnation of hell?"..(Matthew 23:5, 13, 24-25, 27, 33).

Does this upset your image of the gentle Jesus? Can anyone doubt it? Jesus hated religious legalism and hypocrisy. When is the last time you heard a polite pastor deal so firmly with a religious hypocrite?

"Woe unto you scribes, Pharisees, and hypocrites. For you are as graves which appear not, and the men that walk over them are not aware of them" (Luke 11:44). This is a harsh rebuke. Jesus is speaking to men who love to be noticed: to receive respectful greetings in the market place, to be invited to sit at the head of the table. These were men who were impressed with their "holier- than- thou" selves. Because they were so impressed with themselves, they thought others should be impressed too. Jesus was not. He was saying to them the equivalent of, "You are so impressive men don't even notice you. Your religion has rendered you dead while you live and the unimpressed that are forced to tolerate your hypocrisy haven't even bothered to mark your graves."

Take note: Jesus deliberately provoked the legalists of His day. He instigated head on confrontations with them. He refused to tolerate their oppressive influence. He was not nice to them. He continually confronted them and condemned their brand of religion. He never once backed up for it. He had no interest in trying to make peace with it. So why do we? Pastor, why do you tip-toe around it? Don't you know what it is doing behind your back, or maybe in your face? Why are you so reticent to confront the "holier- than- thou" legalists who are laying burdens too heavy to bear on the backs of believers in your church?

Why do you continue passively tolerating a subversive force that pressures and embarrasses your youth with its petty rules and unrealistic dress codes? Do you honestly believe a young girl who attends a public high school should be shamed for wearing jeans or putting on a little make-up? Do you truly believe Jesus is so concerned about enforcing petty rules and ridiculous dress codes that He would subject our Christian youth to so much unnecessary pressure?

It is difficult enough for young people to stand for Christ in this evil age, without the added burdens of mean religion. Once in awhile, I encounter someone from my generation who reveals his ignorance by saying something to the effect, "It's no different than when we were young. We faced the same temptations." That is an incredibly stupid statement. It is different now. Young people weren't taking guns to school and shooting fellow students when I was in high school. We still said the Pledge of Allegiance and even prayed now and then. Some teachers had Bible's on their desks. You could talk about Jesus and not be persecuted by other students. I didn't hang out with Christian kids but I didn't mock them. A young person who openly witnesses today comes under all sorts of pressure.

The whole public educational system seems to be designed to destroy the faith of our Christian youth. They deal with a lot more than evolution being taught as science. The revisionists have managed to edit positive references to God, and His influence on our founders, out of the history books. Evil and temptation like people my age never imagined is in their face every day. Our homes are falling apart. Suicides have increased astronomically. What kind of person would want to increase the pressure by adding petty doctrinal requirements and outrageous dress codes to the mix?

Legalism lays burdens too heavy to bear on the backs of godly young people. It demands that they act and dress in a manner that invites rejection. Our youth are facing enough pressure. They don't need the heavy weight of excessive rules of conduct and dress to make it even more difficult. That old legalist who seems to know the Bible so well will damage your precious children, if you fail to protect them. He may know the Bible but he has not experienced its life. He applies it like the Judaizers; to him it is the letter of the law. God's Word properly understood and applied brings life and liberty, not pressure and bondage.

Young people face more pressure at school everyday than most of us did on our worst day. I want to have enough spiritual intelligence to at least try to understand. I have no tolerance for legalism that calls itself holiness. Religion that majors on externals and insists on ridiculous dress codes for our youth is mean and dumb. It should be rejected by every believer who understands the true nature of holiness, and especially by those who have some sense of the power of peer pressure. Tell the Pharisees to stop laying heavy burdens on our youth. They already have enough on their plates.

Chapter Six

This Snake Has Fangs

Legalism is so spiritually blind it can only see the outside of the cup - not what is in it. It majors on externals. It has clean hands and a dirty heart. How many zealous youth, burning with love for Jesus, have had their fire extinguished by mean religion? Do we need to be reminded that, *"Man looks on the outward appearance. God looks on the heart"* (1 Samuel 16:7). How many Christian youth are now backslidden because we politely tolerated legalism and avoided upsetting the Pharisees among us? How many young men and women, who would have been in the ministry today, are not even attending church because we didn't protect them from the absurdity of small-brained, religious legalism or from the hypocrites who insisted on it?

Jesus was a loving person but He hated religious bondage. Jesus was a polite person but, let me say again, He was not nice to legalists. Should we not follow His example and, if necessary, provoke them in order to expose them? Why don't we make them take off the masks and let people see the snake hiding behind the respectable, religious façade? Legalism is mean. This snake has fangs. The leaven of the Pharisees will kill you. Don't let the masks fool you. The poison can be injected by someone wearing a look of concern, who gives you a sympathetic pat on the back, while he uses his other hand to drop poison in your cup. Don't fall for the "I'm concerned for you brother" charade. A Pharisee is a subtle legalist who wears different faces. The spirit driving him hates you but he may hide behind the face of one thought to be a friend.

We frustrate the grace of God by not exposing and confronting legalism. Legalism rides high on the list of sins Jesus hates. He came to set people free; legalists traffic in bondage. Here is what Jesus had to say about them in Matthew 23:4: *"For they bind heavy burdens, hard to bear, and lay them on men's shoulders...."* If you are a loving pastor, you want to undo the heavy burdens and set people free. Does it make any sense at all to be so polite that you allow legalists to move among your congregation and lay the burdens back on their shoulders? Legalism is a mean sin. Those who impose it on vulnerable believers are the worst kind of sinners; they are hypocrites who themselves don't do what they are demanding of others. Nobody can live under the pressure of legalism masquerading as holiness. Trying to live under it eventually results in one of two outcomes: you become discouraged and give up, or you become frustrated and play the hypocrite. I pray that every loving pastor reading these words will receive the discernment to clearly see the dangers of mean religion and the courage to deal with it.

I also pray for leaders that are trapped in legalistic religion. I am not writing this to attack you. It is clear that Jesus attacked the Pharisees and condemned their hypocrisy. But He didn't launch the attacks to destroy the person with the disease. He was after the infirm religious spirit causing the sickness of legalism. He loved the person but hated the sin. He sincerely wanted to help the person bound by the sin. Jesus would forgive any repentant Pharisee just as He would any other sinner. The problem is that few Pharisees are even willing to entertain the possibility that they are sinners like the lower life forms around them. They are blind to their own sin but have become experts in seeing the sins of others. Jesus exposed and rebuked them, not simply to humiliate or embarrass them, but in the hope that they would see their sin and turn from it. If you see a little of yourself in the following verses it is my prayer that you will humble yourself and repent. Jesus is merciful. Repentance could deliver you, and those you have influenced, from the misery of small-brained, religious legalism.

"And why beholdest the mote that is in thy brother's eye, but considerest not the beam that is in thine own eye? Or how wilt thou say to thy brother, let me pull out the mote out of thine eye;

and, behold, a beam is in thine own eye? Thou hypocrite, first cast out the beam out of thine own eye; and then shalt thou see clearly to cast out the mote out of thy brother's eye" (Matthew 7:3-5).

In language we can better understand, Jesus is saying to the religious hypocrites here: "You can't see the board in your own eye but you can see the splinter in your brother's." Pharisees are so focused on the sins of others that they can't see their own. On the rare occasions when they do, their religious pride helps them find a way to justify it, so they seldom truly repent. Eventually this behavior will result in the loss of all spiritual vision and they will become "blind guides of the blind"

Jesus told another story designed to help a Pharisee realize how messed up he was. Remember, He did it not simply to mock stupidity, but in the hope that the lights would come on and move the proud Pharisee to repentance . *"And He spake this parable unto certain which trusted in themselves that they were righteous, and despised others." Two men went up into the temple to pray; the one a Pharisee, and the other a publican. The Pharisee stood and prayed thus with himself, God, I thank thee that I am not as other men are, extortioners, unjust, adulterers, or even as this publican. I fast twice in the week; I give tithes of all that I possess. And the publican, standing afar off, would not lift up his eyes so much unto heaven, but smote upon his breast, saying, God be merciful to me a sinner. I tell you, this man went down to his house justified rather than the other: for every one that exalteth himself shall be abased; and he that humbleth himself shall be exalted"* (Luke 18:9-14).

This parable is bad news for the Pharisees, but great news for the sinner who humbles himself and repents. Did you notice that God heard the sinner but the Pharisee didn't even get his attention? In verse nine the wording reveals a lot: *"The Pharisee stood and prayed thus with himself...."* God wasn't even listening to him. Religious pride and legalism will make you a spiritual schizophrenic. You will be talking to yourself and think you are carrying on a conversation with someone else. We have big words to describe people who behave that way. A lot of people who talk to themselves, all the while thinking they are carrying on a conversation with others, are on heavy medication or in institutions. The humble sinner had a conversation with God. The proud Pharisee prayed all by himself.

I recently had dealings with a legalistic leader. He is a modern day Judaizer but doesn't even know it. He just thinks he is holier than everyone else. I knew, like the Pharisee in the parable, that this man despised me. But he was too "courteous" to ever say it to my face. He didn't have a problem saying it behind my back though. He justified his gossip, a clear violation of scripture, by telling himself that he was just trying to protect others from my corrupting influence. I challenged his strict belief system which shut people out of heaven and wouldn't even call them saved until they had been baptized in Jesus' name and spoken in other tongues. I also took issue with his petty man-made rules of behavior and dress. My dress code can be summed up with just one word: modesty. His dress code is a bit more complex: For men: hair can't touch your ears or your collar, no beards allowed, no preaching in short sleeve shirts, etc. For women: no jewelry, no make-up, no pants, no cutting hair, no shorts for high school girls who want to play basketball or volleyball, no trimming split ends, ad nauseam. Don't you know that this kind of Christianity will have people lining up to get into our churches?

Chapter Seven

Run While You Can

I have dealt with many hypocrites advanced in the fine art of seeing splinters in the eyes of others. One was a gossiping secretary who I kept on board, in spite of concerns expressed by my wife, because she was efficient and highly productive. That unwise executive decision exacted a painful toll. She later subtly tried to dismantle a church my wife and I planted when we returned from Latin America. She paid tithes like the Pharisees – to the penny. Her tithe checks were numbers like $50.76. She never rounded it up to the next dollar. The beginning of her demise actually started before her actions to destroy the church were revealed. It started when I learned that she was making fun of my seven year old daughter in children's church. My daughter has always been a worshipper. In her younger years, she would sometimes dance and skip around the church during worship services. She often got other children to join her. I loved it. It injected life and excitement into the meetings and it made the services more enjoyable for the children.

Then suddenly she stopped doing it. When I questioned her, I learned that Miss Pharisee had been explaining to her why it was not proper behavior. She considered the activities of excited children a distraction to the service. I explained that the noise and energy of children was not on my list of distractions to worship, but adults who act like children are. I then wasted no time helping that gossiping secretary to "resign" and, thankfully, my wife never once said, "Told you so."

Fortunately, my daughter still loves the Lord and is in ministry today. She has been to several different nations and has served as a missionary in Thailand. She leads worship wherever she goes. Recently, a young woman who had been kidnapped at thirteen and trafficked sexually for seven years, came to a safe-house where my daughter ministers. For two days she wouldn't (or couldn't) speak a word. On the third day my daughter took her keyboard to the home and started singing to the traumatized young woman. She just sat there and stared blankly at her for several minutes, but then she started singing with Brianna, "There is power in the name of Jesus to break every chain..." She has been talking ever since. Had I not protected my daughter from Miss Pharisee, there is a good chance she wouldn't be a worship leader today and that precious young victim might still be staring into space, unable to speak because of the deep pain and paralyzing fear that had ruled her life for so many years.

We underestimate the damage a legalistic Pharisee can do to our precious youth. We are too polite, too tolerant of their ungodly behavior. How many young people will be discouraged from becoming worship leaders or missionaries because pastors refuse to confront the Pharisees who think they have a license to lay heavy burdens on them?

I know this is provocative writing but behind the hard questions is a sincere desire to help. Some of you reading this are not like the hypocrites who impose rules on others which they themselves don't follow. You are already conflicted. You are not at peace with mean religion. You have seen it for what it is: A shadow without substance, a dead thing that robs people of the peace and joy Jesus longs to give them. You have thought about getting away from it but you don't know where to go. You don't know what else you would do. This has been your life. It is all you have known but now you are troubled because you see how messed up it is. My unsolicited advice to you is: Run! Run while you can still think. Run before the religious fog in your brain robs you of the ability to reason. Get away from it, resist it, and don't let it pull you back. You know in your heart that it is not like Jesus.

Once you decide to get out, don't listen to the little voice in your head that says, "Don't leave." Don't listen to the religious devil that plants thoughts like this in your brain: "Now that you have seen it for what it is, you can help others by staying." There is a good chance that if you decide to stay and try to change it, you will be pulled back into it. You will probably have about as much success in that endeavor as the young woman who marries an unbeliever thinking she will be able to convert him once they are married. If you are a pastor, you know the opposite happens more often than not.

It is frightening to walk away from something that you have grown up with and become accustomed to. You may know it is wrong but you feel comfortable in it, and you derive a certain amount of security from it. Anyone remember the cry of the pathetic first generation Israelites? "We want to go back to Egypt." This is co-dependency at its worst. Make up your mind that, no matter how difficult it is to walk away, you are going to break free and stay free. Jesus hates legalism because of what it does to people He loves. We should hate it for the same reason. If you know it is unreasonable, don't leave your children and loved ones to suffer in it. Take time to talk to some broken hearted parents who hated it but were afraid to leave. Ask them how their decision to stay affected their children. Ask them what they would do if they could go back and change that decision.

I know how hard it is to walk away. I was attached to a domineering leader early in my ministry. I thought he was ten feet tall – until I got to know him. Sometimes it seemed that he was on a mission to destroy me. He was critical and judgmental (I don't know if the emphasis should be on the "judge" or the "mental"). It was a bad deal. I had merged my ministry with his. All of my money and assets had been brought in. I endured the abuse longer than I should have, but the day came when I said "Enough" and began making plans to leave.

But then I made a bad mistake. That dictatorial leader also knew how to play the "poor me card." After a lengthy talk with him, I agreed to stay. I actually began to pity him when I realized that he had never matured emotionally. Some unresolved conflict or hurt from his past had made a mess of his emotions. An insecure, frightened little thing was hiding behind the big, strong exterior. I empathized and actually thought that I could help him. (The devil helped me a lot with the demented thinking that brought me to that conclusion). He had the kind of problems that mere human intervention from a concerned young minister cannot fix. The precious time I invested trying to help him was a total waste. He seemed reasonable for about a month but then became worse than ever. A year later he asked me to leave (after slandering me to every leader in the area who would lend an ear). I agreed to leave without causing a stir and without taking anything. But I did ask for his blessing. I learned from Jacob that even old prophets who lean on a staff can say something over you that will release blessing into your life. It is wise to extract blessing out of bitter experience whenever possible.

He was so relieved that I was willing to go without causing trouble or taking anything, he wanted to bless me immediately. I said, "Back up the bus. I want a real blessing – the kind the patriarchs gave. You think about it, pray about it, and I will be in your office tomorrow morning." He took my request seriously. To my anxious to leave ears, his blessing sounded almost as powerful as Jacob blessing his sons. He was so excited "his thorn in the flesh" was leaving peacefully he got carried away. I am still running in the strength of that blessing. He went on in his dogmatic doctrinal way and, a few years later, hit a wall that wouldn't move for him. I went on blessed and full of faith for better days.

Chapter Eight

It's Just Manure, Man

I felt relieved. I left without fear or anxiety, but I did have a few concerns: forty of them. Twenty-two women and eighteen men were in our drug rehabilitation program. In less than two months, we would be without facilities for them. That left little time to make other arrangements. A lot of people were standing around waiting to see me fall on my face. I think some were even selling tickets to the event. But God had other plans. We found property with a couple of old houses that seemed to have potential. Our only problem was that we had no money and little ability to obtain a loan. I still had long hair and a beard and "Jesus Freaks" weren't well thought of by most bankers. To many of them, we were just lazy hippies who found religion. But desperation drove me to rise up with feeble faith and a little confidence and go talk to a banker. I put on my best pair of jeans and my favorite brown T-shirt, and walked into the bank trying my best to act like I expected them to be glad to see me. The loan officer wore a sideways grin throughout most of the application process, but I guess I misread him. He told us if we could make a down payment of $10,000 he would grant the loan.

Truthfully, it might as well have been $100,000. There was no way, humanly speaking, that we could do it. Keep in mind: We were ex-hippies and drug addicts. I, the fearless leader, would have been voted most likely not to succeed in high school. Only God and my mother had not written me off before Jesus changed my life. I was not a good candidate for a loan.

The day of the deadline found me praying in my office before the sun woke up. I had to be at the bank with $10,000 by noon. We had done everything we knew to do but had been able to raise only $5,000. I was still praying when the phone rang at 9:05 A. M. I answered and heard the voice of an 83 year old intercessor who had taken me on as a personal prayer project. Sister Hattie Wattles loved me for leading her favorite nephew to Jesus. She had been a circuit riding Methodist preacher in another lifetime. Now she invested herself in prayer for people like me. "Ronnie, how much money do you need?" I answered, "We are praying and believing God, Sister. She retorted, "That's not the answer to my question. How much money do you need?" For some reason I had trouble spitting it out, but I finally mumbled, "We need $5,000 by noon."

After several "Hallelujahs" and "Praise the Lord's" she said, "Well what are you waiting for? You better get over to Western Union and pick up the money I just wired. The Lord spoke to me at five o'clock this morning to send you $5,000." I had no idea she had that kind of money.

I said all that to say this: Don't be afraid to leave what you now know to be wrong. It may be difficult. You may be bombarded with fiery darts from the enemy. Your wife may wonder how you will make it outside the little religious world you have camped in for so long. But if your eyes have been opened, I encourage you to silence your fears, spit on your doubts and walk away with your head held high. Try to leave with a right spirit but if you are about to saturate the atmosphere of legalism with your absence, I don't advise seeking their blessing as you leave. A lot of people who tried that have been told that hell was waiting outside their walls. But if your eyes have been opened, don't yield to fear or intimidation. Depart wearing the attitude with which the Apostle Paul left the same sort of mess and you will see the blessing of God. *"But what things were gain to me, those I counted loss for Christ. Yea doubtless, and I count all things but loss for the excellency of the knowledge of Christ Jesus my Lord: for whom I have suffered the loss of all things, and do count them but dung, that I may win Christ"* (Philippians 3:7-10).

"…and do count them but dung." It's just manure, man. Leaving is not losing. Don't cry. Get up, get out of the barnyard of mean religion, and get moving. Heaven will come to help you.

Depart like Abraham. It wasn't easy to be Abraham and Sarah. They had to leave all that was comfortable, all that was familiar, friends and family and go out "not knowing where they were going." They left it all behind and launched out on a journey of faith to follow a God they had never seen. They definitely got outside their comfort zone. I challenge every enlightened preacher, still putting up with the foolishness of mean religion, to be like Abraham. Just get up and go. God has something better for you. *"By faith Abraham, when he was called to go out into a place which he should after receive for an inheritance, obeyed; and he went out, not knowing whither he went"* (Hebrews 11:9). Just get up and go in faith leaving the whole package of man-made doctrines and unreasonable rules of dress, doctrine and behavior behind you. Heaven will come to help you.

Don't forget: The devil doesn't like to let people go. He will send someone, or something, to follow you. Be alert and ready for his sinister and subtle temptations. He wants to pull you back. Don't take lightly his ability to come in many different forms. He is a master con with an array of different masks.

Remember, mean spirits sometimes hide behind smiling faces. Don't get caught off guard by the battle that so often follows the departure. A smiling brother can become mean in a moment if you refuse to return to prison with him, or if you confront the religious spirit hiding behind the smile. You will need supernatural strength and resolve to hold your ground. This spirit is not easily overcome. It doesn't respect your opinions. It won't leave you in peace. It will wake you up late at night and try to wear you down in every way possible. But you can win the battle. The Apostle Paul did and your Bible is filled with advice written down by him that tells us how to get free, and how to stay free.

You are at war with mean religion. The battles are often fierce but it is a war worth fighting. The stakes are high. Your stand may mean the difference between a young person pursuing the real Jesus with passion, or leaving the church confused because nobody challenged the Pharisees who misrepresented Him. Most youth exiting our churches aren't rebelling against a relationship with a loving God; they are rejecting a religious system that misrepresents Him.

Chapter Nine

The "Jesus Only" Heresy

Christian legalism comes in many different packages and can be found in many different religious systems and denominations. I will deal primarily here with the system with which I have the most personal experience and which has caused me the most trouble: Pentecostal legalism. Carried to extremes, Pentecostal legalism reduces relationship with Jesus to an external religious ritual. I am a Christian who embraces the experience and the doctrine of the Apostles revealed in the book of Acts and the Epistles; but I reject excessive legalism. It is what Paul encountered in the Judaizers of the first century. The legalists Paul rebuked in the book of Galatians were former Pharisees who had been converted, baptized in the name of Jesus, and filled with the Holy Ghost. Sadly, they brought their oppressive, man-made doctrines and rules with them into Christianity. They were in bondage to a mean, religious spirit and they were driven to infect others with their disease. If you didn't believe what they believed, if you r refused to live by their rules, they labored vigorously to convince you that you were not truly saved.

The pressure was not easy to resist. Even Peter played the hypocrite when the Judaizers came to town. Consider how strong this thing must be; it intimidated both Peter and Barnabas. Peter ate pork chops with the Gentiles until the legalists showed up. When they arrived he acted like a hypocrite and separated himself from the worldly eaters of pork. Even Barnabas was intimidated by them: But Paul was not (Galatians 2:11-15). He, like Jesus, was not nice to legalism. Galatians contains scathing rebukes of this narrow, small-brained brand of Christianity. It made Paul so mad he publicly rebuked Peter for giving in to it. Paul didn't tip-toe around it. If you think he would have put up with the sectarianism and grace-frustrating rules of modern Pentecostal legalism, I challenge you to read the book of Galatians. I pray that those who, like Peter, see its evil but refuse to resist it will be enlightened by Paul's handling of it.

"I marvel that you are so soon removed from him that called you into the grace of Christ unto another gospel... there be some that pervert the gospel of Christ. But though we or an angel from heaven, preach any other gospel unto you...let him be accursed. As we said before, so say I now again, if any man preach any other gospel unto you than that ye have received, let him be accursed" (Galatians 1:6-9).

Paul was no friend of legalism. He was not kind to it. Love is kind, but it is not kind to everything. The modern church is so confused it knows little of the strength of holy love. The seeker-sensitive segment embraces a diluted gospel that won't confront anything. It presses grace almost to the point of lasciviousness (lawlessness). The legalistic segment is filled with believers who don't truly think that Christianity should be so harsh but are too polite, confused or intimidated to confront the legalists that are perverting the gospel of grace. Paul would have been all over both sides of this modern mess.

We need to become better acquainted with the love revealed in the Bible - the love that lived in Jesus and Paul. It is not the polite, soft-spoken little thing that runs from confrontation. It even knows how to be firm and raise its voice when necessary. It holds godly convictions. Love hates. It can be violent with things that hurt what it treasures. Does anyone doubt that Jesus was filled with love? Was He kind to everything He met? No: Not to the devil; not to the Pharisees and hypocrites; not to the demons hiding behind their smirking, "holier-than-thou" faces. Real love speaks the truth – forcefully, if necessary. We have been so debilitated by the diluted gospel preached on Christian television in America today that we think someone who speaks to Pharisees in the manner of Jesus, or to Judaizers in the manner of Paul, is mean-spirited. The truth is, there is nothing mean about love that exposes and confronts that which frustrates the grace of God.

Paul was not kind to the legalism of the Judaizers: *"O foolish Galatians, who hath bewitched you… (Galatians 3:1). "Am I therefore become your enemy because I tell you the truth? They zealously affect you, but not well… (Galatians 4:16-17). "Stand fast therefore in the liberty wherewith Christ has made you free, and be not entangled again with the yoke of bondage" (Galatians 5:1). "Christ is become of no effect to you, whosoever of you are justified by the law; ye are fallen from grace" (Galatians 5:4).*

Again I say, Paul was no friend of legalism. He did not tolerate it, nor was he kind to it. He hated it with holy passion fueled by fervent love. There is a modern brand which, I think, he would hate even more. It is worse than the brand practiced by the Judaizers. It is the heresy of Pentecostal Modalism which misrepresents the true oneness of the Godhead, insists on adherence to exclusive doctrines and imposes extremely strict codes of dress and conduct. It is as mean in its expression, and as heavy in its bondage, as anything the Pharisees and Judaizers carried in their religious bags. It has trapped multitudes in man-made religious systems like United Pentecostalism and Apostolic Oneness sects. Because I believe these groups to be, in the religious sense, "meaner than a junk-yard dog," I will devote some space to their history and beliefs.

The United Pentecostal Church was formed in 1945 in St. Louis. Its headquarters are in Hazelwood, Missouri. It is small in comparison to Pentecostal groups such as the Assemblies of God and the Church of God. Oneness Pentecostals are absolutely convinced that they have it right and everybody else has it wrong. I have heard many of their pastors excuse their smallness by saying, "it is because we preach the truth or because we hold high standards of doctrine." The Church of the New Testament grew rapidly for the very reasons the Modalists use to justify smallness. They preached the truth in power and love and experienced the greatest period of growth in the history of the Church. The truth is that what the "Jesus Only" crowd does preach is not only false but is often delivered in a wrong spirit – a spirit that condemns everything that doesn't agree with it.

The divisiveness and sectarianism of these groups can be traced to their inception: The Oneness Pentecostal movement was conceived by a spirit of division. Its leaders caused a division in the Pentecostal Movement when they refused to turn away from their newborn heresy. They were rigid and pressed several strange doctrines, but the final straw came with their denial of the triune nature of God: They rejected the belief in the

Trinity which had been considered sound doctrine from the earliest days of Church History. The Assemblies of God considered the new doctrine to be heresy and strongly resisted it. They condemned it at their Fourth General Council meeting in 1916. Some of the proponents of the Modalist heresy reacted with anger and immaturity, which resulted in a major division among Pentecostals. They went on to form the General Assembly of the Apostolic Assemblies, which would spawn some of the most divisive sects in the history of the Church.

These sects today are often referred to as "Jesus Only" or "Oneness Pentecostals" because of their teaching of Modalism which denies the Trinity. Orthodox Christianity believes in the "Oneness of God", but not the way the Modalists do. Orthodox Christians believe "God is one" according to Deuteronomy 6:4 but that the one, true and living God has revealed Himself as Father, Son and Holy Spirit. The plurality of the Godhead has been embraced by Orthodox Christianity for nearly two thousand years. The Modalists are the new kids on the block. New things can be good and even exciting, but in light of ample warnings about deception and false doctrine, we should do some serious praying and study before letting go of a doctrine believed from the earliest days of Christianity. Would God really leave us in the dark for so long over something so important? Did all of the great men of God from the Apostle Paul to Martin Luther to Billy

Graham fail to understand what the Modalists claimed to receive by revelation in the early 1900's?

Common sense alone would lead one to conclude that while there is "oneness" in the Godhead, it is not the "Jesus Only" version of the Modalists. Orthodox Christianity teaches that "oneness" has to do with the perfect unity and harmony within the Godhead – that while God has chosen to reveal Himself to us as three persons, He remains one in essence, nature and substance. To embrace the "Jesus Only" teaching of the Modalists, you would have to believe that Jesus was schizophrenic, or that He had multiple personality disorder. Was He talking to Himself when He prayed to the Father? Was he talking about plans to glorify Himself when He said "the Holy Spirit will glorify me?"

Their failure to apply proper Bible Hermeneutics has led to this disturbing misunderstanding of the Godhead and to the contention with Orthodox Christianity. No human can fully comprehend the Godhead. What we do understand has come by revelation of the Spirit. Our finite minds simply are not capable of understanding the Godhead. All we can do is bow to the revelation of God in Creation, and in the person of Jesus. He has revealed Himself to us as Father, Son, and Holy Spirit. We can believe that God is one, as clearly stated in Deuteronomy 6:4, and yet know by revelation that the one, true and living God has revealed His oneness in relationship: Relationship between Father, Son and Holy Spirit. They function together in eternal oneness expressed in love, unity and perfect harmony. The wonder of it all is that a Being so complete, and so fulfilled in harmonious love within the Godhead, would reach out to humans. This great God with a big heart of love wanted a family. I don't know if a Being so complete needed us, but He wanted us. It is mind boggling to understand that believers become members of the royal family and are destined to experience the glory of oneness in relationship with God and with one another.

How do I know that this is our destiny? Jesus prayed that it would be so: *"That they all may be one; as thou, Father, art in me, and I in thee, that they also may be one in us: that the world may believe that thou hast sent me"* (John 17:21). Did Jesus pray in faith? If you believe He did, you can look forward to a wonderful experience of oneness with the Godhead, and with the spiritual family birthed by the intimate love shared by the Godhead.

John 17 contains several verses which refute the idea of "oneness" as it is interpreted by the Modalists (United Pentecostals and Apostolic Oneness groups). Consider how absurd the prayers of Jesus in John 17 would be, if we interpreted oneness as the Modalists do. They believe that Jesus is the Holy Spirit; Jesus is the Father. The result of this twisted belief system is the "Jesus Only" heresy. With such a belief, His prayers would have sounded much differently. I will present the verses as they are written and then give a paraphrase based on the Modalist view.

"I have glorified thee on the earth...And now, O Father, glorify thou me with thine own self with the glory which I had with thee before the world was" (John 17:4-5). Now the "Jesus Only" version: *"I have glorified me on the earth...And now, O Jesus, glorify thou me with mine own self, with the glory which I had with me before the world was."*

" ... and I come to thee , Holy Father, keep through thine own name those whom thou hast given me, that they may be one , as we are" (John 17:11). Now the "Jesus Only" version: *"and I come to me, Holy Jesus, keep through mine own name those whom I have given me, that they may be one as me is."*

Let's look at verse 21 again, and also verses 22-25: *"That they all may be one; as thou Father, art in me, and I in thee, that they also may be one in us: that the world may believe that thou hast sent me. "And the glory which thou gavest me I have given them; that they may be one, even as we are one: I in them, and thou in me, that they may be made perfect in one; and that the world may know thou has sent me, and hast loved them, as thou hast loved me. Father, I will that they also, whom thou hast given me, be with me where I am; that they may behold my glory, which thou hast given me: for thou lovest me before the foundation of the world. O righteous Father, the world hath not known thee; but I have known thee, and these have known that thou hast sent me."* Now the "Jesus Only" version: *"And the glory which I gavest me I have given them; that they may be one, even as I am one. I in them, and I in me, that they may be made perfect in one; and that the world may know I have sent me, and hast loved them, as I hast loved me. Jesus, I will that they also, whom I hast given me, be with me where I am; that they may behold my glory, which I hast given me: for I lovest me before the foundation of the world. O righteous Jesus, the world hath not known me; but I have known me, and these have known that I hast sent me."*

It gets a bit confusing, doesn't it? It is not only confusing, it is divisive. If we are to be one, as Jesus and the Father are one then I suppose Modalism, followed to its illogical conclusion, will say: I am you and you are me. We are not distinct; we are one person. Thankfully, there is a distinction of personalities. You are you and I am me. Let's not confuse ourselves with ourselves.

That is even more confusing, isn't it? It hurts my head just to discuss it. True "oneness" does not do away with the distinction of personalities in the Godhead. Jesus spoke and prayed often to His Father. Some Modalists say that, in cases such as John 17 and in the Garden of Gethsemane (Matthew 26:36-46), it was the human Jesus calling on the Father in Him. Any thinking person, whose brain has not been infused with religious fog, will quickly realize how absurd that idea is. Try reading the whole New Testament with the goal of noting all the instances where Jesus spoke to, or about, His Father or the Holy Spirit. More often than not, the light of revelation will penetrate your spirit and your brain, and you will part ways with "Jesus Only" heresy of Modalism.

I don't want to spend too much time here discussing the nature of the Godhead. I raise the issue because bad doctrine is often the foundation of mean religion. "Jesus Only" teaching is not sound doctrine. Most of the groups associated with it hold to a "Bible Standard of Salvation" that looks nothing like the standard embraced by orthodox Christianity for over two thousand years. It denies justification through faith and adds works to the Gospel. It insists that a person is not saved until he is baptized in Jesus name and speaks with other tongues. To these requirements is added a rigid system of rules which governs dress and behavior. This is one of the most judgmental and exclusive groups in the history of the church.

Modalists are extremely contentious over the formula used in baptism. Jesus instructed His disciples to baptize in the name of the Father, Son and Holy Ghost. The Father, Son and Holy Ghost were revealed to us in the person of Jesus. The Apostles baptized in the name of Jesus throughout the book of Acts. They were obeying what Jesus commanded in Matthew 28. But the "Jesus Only" groups have argued this to the point of complete unreasonableness. They argue for the right formula so intensely that they often lose sight of the most important factors in baptism. Is the candidate for baptism truly born again? Does he understand that baptism symbolizes death to his old way of life and resurrection to a new life as an obedient disciple of Jesus Christ? If the person being baptized and the person baptizing him are truly born again, it would seem ludicrous to believe that the words spoken as the new believer is immersed could mean the difference between heaven or hell. I just can't see God being that narrow. If we are truly born again through faith in Jesus, everything we do is by His authority and in His name: *"And whatsoever ye do in word or deed, do all in the name of the Lord Jesus..." (Colossians 3:17).*

It is clear that the Apostles baptized in the name of Jesus in the book of Acts. But, if someone follows the formula of Matthew 28 and baptizes in the name of the Father, Son and Holy Ghost, is it necessary to divide over it? Is the formula really the issue, or is it more important to understand that we are baptizing by the authority of the name of Jesus? Why can't all the bases be covered without strict adherence to a certain formula? Why not say something like this: "By the authority of the Lord Jesus Christ, I baptize you in the name of the Father, Son and Holy Ghost." I would have no problem here because we all know that God revealed Himself as Father, Son, and Holy Ghost in the person of Jesus. Why not just do both – what Jesus said in Matthew 28 and what the early believers did in the Book of Acts?

What would be wrong with covering all the bases by just saying, "I baptize you in the name of the Father, Son and Holy Ghost by the authority of and in the name of Jesus? I am willing to accommodate someone who feels the need to be re-baptized, but I would never insist that those who have been truly born again through faith in Jesus, and who understand that their baptism was carried out in obedience to and by the authority of Jesus, be re-baptized using a different formula. I believe that what Jesus commanded in Matthew 28 and what the Apostles did in the book of Acts are one and the same. I don't want to spend precious time fighting over formulas.

Jesus could have used the same wording in Matthew 28 as was used in the book of Acts. If you believe that the translators got it right, you have to believe that Jesus deliberately chose to use different words than those of the Apostles who followed His instructions throughout the book of Acts. I don't know why He did, but the mere fact that He did leads me to believe that Jesus may not be nearly as concerned about formulas as we are.

I know of a missionary who got so fed up with arguments over this issue he simply asked candidates for baptism, "Are you truly born again through faith in Jesus and are you committed to live in obedience to Him?" If they answered in the affirmative, he spoke these words as he immersed them, "I kill you in the name of Jesus" and these words as he lifted them from the water, "I raise you to walk in newness of life." I know of another pastor who says, "I bury you in the name of Jesus and I raise you to walk in fellowship with the Father, Son and Holy Ghost." He tells those he baptizes: "If someone asks you if you were baptized in Jesus' name say, "Yes." And if someone asks you if you were baptized in the name of the Father, Son and Holy Ghost say, "Yes." He doesn't believe that Christians should fight over formulas. It sounds too much like the Pharisees who strained at gnats and swallowed camels.

Chapter Ten

The Plurality and Oneness of the Godhead

The "Jesus Only" crowd makes no distinction between God the Father, God the Son and God the Holy Spirit. In the "oneness belief system, they are all just different manifestations of Jesus. A deficient understanding of hermeneutics has led the Modalists to discount a huge portion of Scripture while insisting on adherence to just a few verses. They deny the plurality of the Godhead which is clearly taught throughout the Bible. They are dogmatic and legalistic in their insistence on adherence to a few isolated texts. They ignore basic rules of interpretation and refuse to consider a larger body of scripture which contradicts their narrow views. Here are just a few of the passages which support the long-held belief of plurality in the Godhead (Genesis 1:26; Matthew 3:16-17; 28:19-20; Mark 1:9-11; John 8:17-18; 14:16; 15:26; 16:13-15; 2 Corinthians 13:14; Ephesians 2:18; 1 Peter 1:2).

"In the beginning God created the heaven and the earth" (Genesis 1:1). "And God said; Let us make man in our image, after our likeness..." (Genesis 1:26). The Hebrew word for God in these verses is 'Elohim'. It is a plural noun. It is used over 2,000 times in the Hebrew Scriptures. Does it imply plurality in

the Godhead? Does this plurality support the orthodox doctrine of the Trinity? Does God exist in perfect oneness as God the Father, God the Son, and God the Holy Spirit? Why do the Modalists refuse to acknowledge this revelation of the oneness of the Godhead? It is a beautiful thought: One God – one in essence, nature and substance – existing in perfect love, unity and harmony as Father, Son, and Holy Spirit. This takes nothing away from Jesus. Yet, the "Jesus Only" groups are totally closed to this beautiful picture of a loving God existing as three distinct personalities in perfect oneness.

They don't dispute that the name of the Creator, Elohim, is plural in Hebrew. But they argue that God was talking to "the sons of God" which are mentioned in isolated passages in the book of Job. Some argue that the "sons of God" were angels who were involved in Creation. This idea cannot be supported when proper rules of hermeneutics are followed and scripture is compared with scripture. The same plural form of God, "Elohim," is used in over 2000 instances that have nothing to do with Creation, and which make no reference to the sons of God. Why, in light of so many verses which use the plural form when mentioning God, is it so difficult to believe that the *"Let us"* of Genesis 1:26 refers to the Father, Son and Holy Spirit?

The plural form of "El" (Elohim) occurs in only one Semitic language: Hebrew. But the idea of plurality in the Godhead has been vigorously disputed since the Modalists came along in the early 1900's. The traditional Hebrew view is that the plural "Elohim" is the name of God used most often as Creator and Judge. It is the standard Hebrew term for Deity. In Creation in Genesis 1:1 and 2:6, it implies majesty in the fullness of Deity. There is nothing here to support the Modalist position that God was speaking to angels in Genesis1:26. Scripture is clear that we are made in God's image, not the image of angels. In Genesis 11:7, *"Us"* is the plural "Elohim" in Hebrew. It seems that the members of the Godhead are conversing with one another and saying, *"Let us go down."* The "Jesus Only" view would require us to believe that, in this passage and in many others, Jesus is talking to Himself.

There are different compound constructs of "Elohim" throughout the Bible. We can't look at all 2,570 of them but we will consider a few. In Isaiah 45:18, the plural "Elohim" is mentioned in relation to Creation. There is no mention of the angels here, or in countless other references that mention "Elohim" in the context of Creation. *"For thus saith the LORD that created the heavens; God himself that formed the earth and made it; he hath established it, he created it not in vain, he formed it to be inhabited: I am the LORD; and there is none else."* The plural "Elohim" is also used in Isaiah 54:5. The "sons of God" are also absent in this verse. *"For thy Maker is thine husband; the LORD of hosts is his name..."*

A few of the compound constructs follow:
*Ben Elohim – The Son of God (Matthew 16:16)
*Elohei Ma'Uzzi –The God of my strength(2 Samuel 22:3233)
*Elohei Mikkarov and Elohei Merachuk – The God who is near and far (Jeremiah 23:23-24)
*Elohei Mishpat – The God of Justice (Isaiah 30:18)
*Elohei Kedem – The eternal God (Deuteronomy 33:27) *Elohim Chayim – The living God (Daniel 6:25-27; Hebrews 9:14)
*Elohim HaAv – God the Father (John 6:27; 1 Corinthians 8:6; Galatians 3:3; Ephesians 6:23; Philippians 2:11; 1 Thessalonians 1:1; 2 Timothy 1:2; Titus 1:4: 1 Peter 1:2-5; 2 Peter 1: 16-18; 2 John 1:3; Jude 1:1-3)

The Bible is filled with evidence supporting plurality in the Godhead. The Modalistic "Jesus Only" crowd is the new kid on the block. This divisive, unorthodox brand of Christianity is constructed on a few isolated, misinterpreted and misapplied texts which cannot hold water against the backdrop of scriptural revelation or Church History. Numerous passages emphasize distinction of function and person between the Father, Son and Holy Spirit. In John 14:25-26, we find Jesus speaking to His disciples, telling them that the Father will send the Holy Spirit to them. In John 16:25-28, we see several clear distinctions Jesus makes between Himself and the Father:

"I will show you plainly the Father"
   "I say not unto you I will pray the Father for you"
   "For the Father himself loveth you, because ye have loved me, and have believed that I came out from God"
   "I came forth from the Father, and am come into the world: again, I leave the world, and go to the Father"

All four Gospels record the baptism of Jesus: (Matthew 3:16-17; Mark 1:10-11; Luke 3:22; John 1:32-34). All but John show Jesus in the water, the Spirit descending in the form of a dove and the Father speaking from heaven. It is implied in John's Gospel. The evidence against the "Jesus Only" concept of oneness is overwhelming. Rather than contemplate their twisted interpretation, much less let them draw you into argument, one should simply scratch his head and wonder how anyone could hold this narrow view against the backdrop of Scripture and Church history. Even Colossians 2:9, a verse which they use as bedrock for their divisive religious system, militates against this position: *"For in him dwelleth all the fullness of the Godhead bodily."* There is clear distinction of persons in their favorite verse: Jesus and the Godhead dwelling in Him.

1 John 5:7 alone should silence all the arguments of the "Jesus Only" sect: *"For there are three that bear record in heaven, the Father, the Word and the Holy Ghost: and these three are one."* Against the backdrop of thousands of verses which support plurality in the Godhead, it is absurd to take the narrow position of the Modalists and interpret "one" in this verse in a mathematical sense as one person. A study of Hebrew writings clearly reveals the belief, throughout the Old Testament, that One God exists eternally in plurality in the Godhead. Some scholars point out that 1 John 5:7 does not appear in original Greek manuscripts. But one would be hard-pressed to find a commentator who questions its authenticity or veracity. Some commentators assert that a more accurate translation is, *"these three agree in one."* That is the whole point of the verse, when taken in its proper context and when viewed in comparison to the countless verses which show plurality in the Godhead. What is being said here is three – Father, Son and Holy Ghost – agree in perfect unity on one testimony: Jesus, the Son of God, is the Messiah. "One" here, as in other places throughout Scripture, should be understood as one in unity and agreement, one in essence, nature or substance. 1 John 5:7-12 emphasizes the unity of a trinity of persons in one Godhead.

The Modalists came late to the table, with aberrant views of oneness, and they remain lonely in the midst of the multitudes of Orthodox Christianity who, instead of hurting their finite brains trying to comprehend the Godhead, simply bow to the revelation God has given us of Himself: One God revealed as three persons – Father, Son and Holy Ghost.

The doctrine of the Trinity is included in every major creed in the history of Christendom. It did not, as some erroneously assert, come out of the Councils of early Christianity. What was already accepted as doctrine was merely penned by some of the early church fathers who participated in the Councils. The concept of the triune nature of the one true God was written on the hearts of the disciples before it ever appeared on paper. There is nothing in the New Testament or Church history that indicates that plurality in the Godhead was questioned. I suspect that one would be hard-pressed to find a handful of heretics, prior to the Modalist departure from sound doctrine in the early 1900's, who would have questioned the revelation of the triune God to man as Father, Son and Holy Spirit. The authors of the New Testament and the leaders of the early Church embraced the triune nature of God. The early Church Councils simply gave the name "Trinity" to the understanding and wrote it into the Creeds. The Apostles' Creed gives no hint of any thought of Modalism in the early Church:

"I believe in God, the Father almighty, Creator of Heaven and Earth. I believe in Jesus Christ, His only Son, our Lord. He was conceived by the power of the Holy Spirit and born of the Virgin Mary. He suffered under Pontius Pilate, was crucified, died, and was buried. He descended into hell. On the third day he rose again. He ascended into Heaven, and is seated at the right hand of the Father. He will come again to judge the living and the dead. I believe in the Holy Spirit, the holy catholic (universal) Church, the communion of saints, the forgiveness of sins, the resurrection of the body, and the life everlasting. Amen."

Chapter Eleven

A Little Leaven Contaminated a Lot of Bread

The United Pentecostal and Apostolic Oneness Churches would have been marked as heretical by the Apostles and early Church fathers. They are among the most divisive sects in the history of Christianity. The amount of trouble brought on the Church as a result of the actions of a few Pentecostal leaders in the early 1900's is astounding. A little leaven contaminated a lot of bread. These sects of the Pentecostal Church have been plagued by a self righteous, divisive spirit since their inception. It is not unlike the legalism of the Judaizers with whom Paul contended. Ignore or underestimate its influence and you will soon discover that it has harmed the most vulnerable in your congregation. It comes with a proselytizing spirit which has great difficulty winning its own converts. Why would we want to give it unchecked access to ours? Jesus and Paul didn't put up with it. Why do we?

You may be one of those who leave it alone because you know it is drying up and diminishing in numbers. But is that wise? Should we surrender even one new Christian to this mean religion which sinks the soul under the heavy weight of bondage to spurious doctrines and petty codes of conduct and dress? It is mean religion which demands that its strict codes of dress and conduct be followed. Failing to adhere is a ticket to hell. It condemns anyone who doesn't believe its strict doctrinal code. It is too dangerous to ignore. Let it die, but don't stand passively by and let it take others with it.

Ronald Reagan said that communism would cave in on itself because the seeds of destruction were built into it from its inception. But he didn't stand idly by and wait for its death. He actively and consistently brought pressure to bear upon it. We should treat Modalism in the same manner; it should not be ignored. A snake, curling and thrashing in the throes of death may seem harmless, but it can still bite you. The Bible charges sincere leaders to *"...mark them which cause divisions and offences contrary to the doctrine which you have learned; and avoid them"* (Romans 16:17).

You can't avoid them if they are trying to drag believers you are responsible for into their dungeons of dead religion. If they come into your sphere of influence, treat them like Paul did. His attitude toward them and dealings with them are clearly revealed in the book of Galatians. He not only went after the Judaizing James and his comrades, he publicly rebuked Peter and Barnabas for coming under their influence. Pastors who know better, yet have ignored the Modalists in their midst, should read

Galatians and follow his example. Why should we allow these hypocritical, white-washed sepulchers to contaminate one more vulnerable believer with their brand of dried up legalism? It is not wise to be nice to mean religion.

A father was taking a hike with his son in a park near my home when he came across a deadly timber rattler. He killed the snake and an animal rights advocate called the police. The man went to jail but he and his son lived to tell about their ordeal. The animal rights advocate said that the proper thing to do would have been to use a walking stick to guide the snake off the path. Many pastors treat legalistic religious snakes the same way. I am in the snake killer's corner. I would rather be called mean-spirited and alive than polite and dead. Give me the chance, and I will kill the snake.

The problem is more than a disagreement over the nature of the Godhead. Bad theology spawns mean religion with its twisted doctrines and petty rules. A.W. Tozer said that "the Trinity is an incomprehensible mystery." He was not numbered among the diminishing adherents of small-brained religion. His brain was big enough to embrace the revelation of the Trinity even though he was incapable of understanding it. The Trinity is revealed not merely in words but in actions and interactions of the Triune God in redemption and in relationship to the redeemed.

Many more verses add weight to this long-held doctrine which the Modalists perverted back in 1914. I have my own ideas as to why the early leaders of Modalism created an aberration of the long held belief in the plurality of the Godhead: Is it not possible that power hungry, unethical leaders used division, created by twisted doctrine, to form their own organization? It certainly wouldn't be the first time in Church History that leaders with a lust for control employed such tactics. We should be cautious before dispensing with a doctrine which has prevailed for 1900 years of Church History. "Jesus Only" Modalism is the new kid on the block. It is hard to imagine how a handful of divisive Pentecostal preachers could do a better job of formulating sound doctrine than all the brilliant minds and great spirits which preceded them. We would be wise to stop trying to understand the Godhead (our finite little brains aren't up to the challenge) and simply bow to the revelation God has given: He has spelled Himself out in the person of Jesus in a language we can understand – the language of love. He has revealed Himself in the person of Jesus as Father, Son and Holy Spirit. You can torture your brain trying to figure it out, or you can simply bow to revelation and enjoy the incredible blessing of being one with Jesus through faith by the mysterious work of the Holy Spirit. Following are just a few of the verses which support the plurality of the Godhead: The belief of New Testament Christians, the early Church Councils, and great men and women throughout Church history.

"And Jesus, when He was baptized, went up straightway out of the water: and lo the heavens were opened unto him, and He saw the Spirit of God descending like a dove, and lighting upon him: And lo a voice from heaven, saying, this is my beloved Son, in whom I am well pleased" (Matthew 3:16-17). Jesus in the water, the Holy Spirit descending, the Father speaking from heaven: You have to violate Hermeneutics and read into the text to say this is just three manifestations of Jesus. There is absolutely nothing that supports this idea. The Modalists are as careless as the cults in their violations of simple Bible interpretation.

"Go ye therefore, and teach all nations, baptizing them in the name of the Father, and of the Son, and of the Holy Ghost" (Matthew 28:19-20). God – Father, Son and Holy Spirit - revealed Himself to us in the person of Jesus. Acknowledging the plurality of the Godhead takes nothing away from Jesus. We can't know God apart from Jesus. All we do in the Kingdom of God, we do in the name of and by the authority of Jesus. He is *"the brightness of God's glory and the express image of His person..." (Hebrews 1:3).* "In Him dwells all the fullness of the

Godhead bodily" (Colossians 2:9). This verse, used by the Modalists to argue their "Jesus Only" position actually does the opposite. A distinction is made between Jesus and the Godhead dwelling in Him. No human brain can fully understand the nature of the Godhead, but it is fairly simple for anyone with a solid grasp of Scripture and a basic understanding of hermeneutics to refute the "Jesus Only" position.

"It is also written in your law, that the testimony of two men is true. I am one that bear witness of myself, and the father that sent me beareth witness of me" (John 17:18). This verse alone should end the argument. A proponent of Oneness would have to at the very least become "two-ness" based on its clear meaning. It reveals plurality in the Godhead.

"And I will pray the Father and He shall give you another Comforter that He may abide with you forever" (John14:16). *"But when the Comforter has come, whom I will send unto you from the Father..."* (John15:26).

My favorite verse supporting this subject is Ephesians 2:18, *"For through Him (Jesus) we both have access by one Spirit unto the Father."* This verse not only shows difference in function but distinction in the persons of the Godhead. If Jesus is the Father, is the Holy Spirit, why would such language be used? We must stop trying to figure out the Godhead with our finite minds and simply bow to God's revelation of Himself to us as Father, Son, and Holy Spirit. There are many verses (too numerous to reference here) which support plurality in the Godhead.

Modalists, and many so-called holiness Pentecostal groups, grossly misrepresent the "Liberating Jesus" of the Bible and replace Him with a harsh taskmaster. They hide legalism behind claims of holiness. Holiness and legalism are not the same thing: Legalism is mean and produces death; holiness is beautiful in its expression and it produces life. Groups that require members to adhere to ridiculous dress codes are often practicing legalism, not holiness. In some circles, it is not only a sin for women to cut their hair; it is a sin to trim split-ends (hello to buns and top-knots).   Legalism often forbids the wearing of jewelry, pants or make-up. These male dominated hierarchies are not as hard on men, but requirements for them can still be quite weird: no hair over the ears or touching the collar; you dare not preach in a short-sleeved shirt; if you grow a beard you may be judged not simply "unshaved" but "unsaved".

Chapter Twelve

Get Your Own Converts

I love Pentecostal power. I hate Pentecostal legalism. I always endeavored to move in Pentecostal power when witch-doctors came to put curses on me in my crusades throughout Africa; legalism would not have impressed them. There is no power to liberate in legalism. Like witchcraft, it brings people under bondage and controls them with fear. Embrace it and, in record time, you will also be breathing the polluted air of mean religion. Leave the door open for it long enough and you will be in danger of coming under the same bondage as the preacher who came into your midst packing it. I have listened to legalistic preachers condemn men for wearing short sleeve shirts to church, for growing beards, or wearing their hair a little too long. I have heard them condemn women for wearing jewelry, make-up or, God forbid, pants.

Paul dealt with legalism in the book of Galatians. It is not difficult to perceive how much he hated it. If anyone understood the deceptive nature and danger of legalism, it was the Apostle Paul. Before his conversion he was a strict Pharisee. He lived for many years in the bondage of mean religion. He became as mean as his religion and was the leading persecutor of the first

Christians. But when he met Jesus on the road to Damascus, he found freedom from religious bondage. From that day forward he waged warfare against legalism and bondage. His language toward it is harsh in all of his writings, especially in the book of Galatians. There is no doubt that Paul advocated for liberty in Christ, not bondage under rules and regulations. He knew the difference between legalism and holiness.

In 1979, I established a church and missionary training school in San Antonio, Texas. I spent many Friday and Saturday nights distributing gospel tracts downtown and on the River Walk. On one of those outreaches, I encountered a "holiness" preacher who was distributing tracts titled, "Why God Hates Mini-Skirts." I confronted him with the sincere hope of helping him come out of the fog. But he was a mile wide and an inch deep. That guy convinced me that ignorance and shallowness must be second cousins. It is difficult to reason with both of them at the same time – even if you are open to help from the spiritual gifts of wisdom and knowledge. I won't bore you with his defense; it was more pathetic than the tract. I asked him things like "What in God's name are you thinking" and, "Man, what are you smoking?" The truth is, he wasn't thinking. Thinking is hard work. That is why so few people do it; but in a glorious exercise of futility, I tried to get "Mr. Holiness Preacher" to think. I reasoned: "These are rebellious teens; some are hardened gang members; there are drug addicts and prostitutes in the mix. Should we not just tell them "Jesus loves you" up front and leave them alone long enough to let the Holy Spirit change what he wants to in their dress and behavior?" My experience has been that most girls who get saved stop wearing mini-skirts after a while anyway - without any help from the legalists who want women to wear dresses that cover their ankles

I am not writing this to embarrass those who have done dumb things. I have been a little less than intelligent myself a few times. I am not writing this to infuriate the Pharisees or the Judaizers. I just want to expose what is hiding behind their religion. I sincerely want to help those in bondage. I still have hope that the lights might come on. I also want to rescue some of the captives who are being held prisoner by mean religion – especially those locked up in the dungeons of the Modalists.

United Pentecostalism and Apostolic Oneness are sectarian and exclusive. Those who do not hold to every tenet of their "Bible Standard of Salvation" are shut out of heaven. To be saved one must: Repent of sin, receive Jesus by faith, be baptized by immersion in the name of Jesus, and be baptized in the Holy Ghost with the evidence of speaking in other tongues. Missing it on one point condemns you. This perversion of the gospel puts every great man and woman of God who never spoke in other tongues in hell. Why do we tolerate it? Why are we polite to it? Why do we let it testify in our meetings or stand it up behind our pulpits and give it a microphone? Do we really want to continue giving place to something wicked enough to put Billy Graham in hell?

Is it any wonder that in this small-brained belief system, new converts become frustrated and leave the church with heads hanging down, because they just can't seem to get a release in tongues? Why do they think that way: Because we allowed some legalist to steal their new-found freedom and joy with oppressive, man-made doctrines. It is utter abdication of loving leadership to allow demented Pharisees to break new believers down with truck loads of man-made rules and doctrines. How many excited new believers went to an altar to pray for the fullness of the Spirit, and left condemned because some Pharisee told them they weren't saved until they spoke in other tongues? Why do those of us who hate this foolishness allow them to minister at our altars? We tolerate things that should have been dealt with long ago.

I remember a tent revival where I was one of several evangelists. God's blessing was on the meetings and we continued from July to October. We witnessed healings, salvation, and people being filled with the Spirit. One night I was praying at the altar after a powerful message by a young evangelist. Next to me was a young man who had been born again a few weeks before. He had found the peace and joy of Jesus. He was filled with the excitement of a new believer. But that night something was different. He seemed to have the weight of the world on his shoulders. I heard him praying "Jesus please save me." I put my hand on his shoulder and said, "Brother, I thought you had already received Jesus. He responded, "I thought so, too, but I just can't get a release in tongues."

Upon further questioning, I discovered that a modern Judaizer had done this to him. Guys like him move about from church to church and revival to revival trying to "enlighten" other people's converts. They may not be fully cognizant of their mission, but what they are attached to is wide awake. They have ample time on their hands and just sit around waiting for some new convert to instruct, or some young preacher to counsel. They mess with other people's converts: Modalism at its best: Why don' they go get their own?

It is an ugly aberration of the glorious gospel that tells people they are not saved until they talk in other tongues. This kind of religion drives people back to the world completely frustrated, holds them in bondage to a hypocritical religious system, or causes them to leave disgusted with all the rules. In reaction to the petty rules and exclusive doctrines, such victims often end up embracing a diluted gospel of grace carried to the point of lawlessness: the other side of the pendulum.

Nobody can live long under Pentecostal legalism. They either leave it or become self righteous and hypocritical – just like the Pharisees and the Judaizers who preceded them. The unbearable internal conflict and frustration produced by this heavy-handed religion will let you exist miserably, but it robs you of the joy of real life. It fools you into thinking that emotional outbursts and fleshly demonstrations are manifestations of Holy Ghost life and power. More often than not, they are just pressure being released from over-burdened souls who don't know what else to do when moved to states of religious frenzy. The feelings often subside as soon as the music stops. This mean religion often produces "meeting junkies" who are always looking for an atmosphere conducive to administering another fix. In these circles, much that is called a manifestation of the Holy Ghost is just excited religious flesh trying to find a few moments of relief.

Chapter Thirteen

All Hat and No Cowboy

I embrace the real Jesus wherever I find Him. I have tried to avoid contention and division over different views of the Godhead. I seek common ground whenever possible. But, through the years, I have come to understand how difficult that is. Those who embrace the "Jesus Only" view seem obsessed with the need to convince everyone else that they are wrong. I don't think anyone truly understands the Godhead but my "oneness" friends are convinced that they do. I have encouraged them often to stop trying to figure it out and simply bow to God's revelation of Himself to us. He has revealed Himself in Creation and in Jesus. He has revealed Himself as one God manifest as Father, Son and Holy Spirit. Jesus called on His Father in prayer continually. He relied on the Holy Spirit completely. Their interaction reveals oneness expressed in plurality.

Truthfully, the intimate love and spiritual oneness of the Godhead is so mind-blowing, it is beyond human ability to comprehend mentally. The only way we will ever get it is by revelation. We are only able to comprehend what God graciously reveals to us in His word, in Jesus and by the precious Holy Spirit. Because it is so difficult for us to comprehend, I think it is futile to argue over different views. If a person believes that Jesus is the only way to know God, and claims to have a relationship with Him on that basis, why not try to have fellowship around truths we hold in common? Sadly, I must admit that in my experience this has been nearly impossible. It is difficult to have mature dialogue with dogmatic believers who are so convinced that they are right they aren't even polite enough to listen to your point of view. Their mission is to convince you that you are wrong and they often become rude and argumentative when their narrow views are questioned. When someone who is well-grounded in scripture intelligently challenges their position they often respond with volume and anger – marks of uncertainty and immaturity. A person can be so right he is wrong – wrong in spirit.

Sound doctrine should produce maturity of character and thought. It should result in the developing of the fruit of Spirit which produces a desire to embrace others in love, not reject them or shut them out because they refuse to agree with our doctrinal position. It can be difficult to try to reason with a legalist. When there is any kind of exchange of ideas, they are not really listening with interest to what you have to say. They are just waiting for an opportunity to argue their position. They are obsessed with one purpose: to enlighten you by arguing until you give up and come around to their way of thinking. They are so convinced of their "rightness" and your "wrongness" it becomes extremely difficult to walk in any kind of agreement with them.

Sectarian spirits often attach themselves to divisive doctrinal systems. The spirit driving this rigid system of legalism won't allow its adherents to embrace or endeavor to keep the unity of the Spirit for which Paul advocates in Ephesians 4:3. Division is the air they breathe. Modalism was born in division and the whole system is shot-through with its destructive influence. This movement is rife with self righteous, religious spirits which work harder trying to make proselytes of Christians with different belief systems than it does trying to win the lost. I have purposed to be patient but I have grown weary of its continual subterfuge.

A recent meeting with pastors caused me to resolve to treat this spirit with the kind of disdain Jesus and Paul demonstrated toward it. I had previously conducted several great meetings with a group of pastors, but then a modern Judaizer attended one of them. The atmosphere was totally different. I sensed tension in the air the moment I walked through the door. He floated the idea that I had corrupted the doctrine of a pastor in the group who had climbed over the foreboding walls of mean religion to come into the light of a bigger world.

I later learned that Mr. Legalist had talked with three of the pastors before the meeting. This is common behavior for legalists. Those who are insecure and deficient in real spiritual authority often try to find strength in numbers. He thought he could ambush me with the help of those he had talked to before the meeting. When he began expressing his concerns by asking contentious questions, I responded with several scriptures memorized long ago. I have dealt with this thing all over the world. Its arguments have always been narrow, shallow and boring. They are easily refuted by any student of the Bible with even an elementary understanding of hermeneutics. I confronted him with truth spoken firmly but, hopefully, in love. For the sake of the pastors I had been teaching, I felt compelled to refute his narrow doctrinal assertions but I sincerely wanted to help him.

I have nothing against such men but I am at war with what they are attached to. Sometimes people become so miserable in this law based, rule driven system, they come to a point where they are open to reason. Astute leaders should be willing to do all that is possible to help a soul in bondage at those moments. The man I described a little earlier does not fit the belligerent, domineering prototype of many legalistic leaders. Men like him sometimes wake up to the bondage they are living under when they are firmly confronted with truth. It can be frustrating to try to help people trapped in legalism but, when given the opportunity, we should try. Because their arguments are often presented with the false pride that accompanies insecurity, dialogue can be difficult. But sometimes listening with patience and discernment can result in revelation that brings release.

Some who are oppressed by legalism want out of its prison but are afraid that hell waits outside the walls. That is what leaders of cults and oppressive religious organizations try to get their followers to believe. They are brainwashed into thinking: "We are right and everyone else is wrong. If you are not obedient and faithful to uphold our standard, you are condemned." Such people are ruled by the fear of failing to make it. The possibility of losing salvation is continually held over their heads. They are deceived by an oppressive religion of works and don't even realize it. We must not write them off as hopeless. Their only hope of escape is truth spoken in love and grace that does not depend on salvation by works.

I must admit that I have been frustrated trying to deal with many "oneness" leaders. It takes humility and repentance for a legalist to come out of the fog. Insecurity and pride often result in "hardening of the attitudes." Legalism is a spiritual sickness. I know because I had a case of it for a season. I wish someone would have diagnosed my disease. I wish someone would have recognized it and prescribed medicine in the early stages. Unfortunately, I had to figure it out myself and by the time I did others had been infected; legalism is contagious. Fortunately, I found medicine like Romans 8:1, *"There is therefore now no condemnation to them which are in Christ Jesus, who walk not after the flesh but after the Spirit."* Regular does of verses like Galatians 5:1 have also helped me resist the return of the disease: *"Stand fast therefore in the liberty wherewith Christ hath made us free, and be not entangled again with the yoke of bondage."*

After escaping from the dungeon of legalistic religion, I had no desire to be infected again with the debilitating disease. But in the early period of my freedom, the devil often sent agents to try to re-infect me with viruses like intimidation and fear. To resist such viruses and stay free, we must reinforce our spiritual immune system and build ourselves up in the Word and the Spirit. Taking daily supplements of verses like Romans 5:1-2 is essential: *"Therefore being justified by faith, we have peace with God through our Lord Jesus Christ: By whom also we have access into this grace wherein we stand, and rejoice in hope of the glory of God."* Remembering that authentic Christianity is "grace based" helps us resist legalism and "letter of the law" religion. The practice of daily spiritual exercise is also helpful. Here is a good one: *"But ye beloved, building up yourselves on your most holy faith, praying in the Holy Ghost"* (Jude 20). You can stay free of legalism. The Bible is filled with medicine, supplements and exercises to make you strong enough to resist and overcome it totally. In fact, diligent study and application of Scripture, coupled with daily dependence on the Holy Spirit, will equip you to set others free.

However, no matter how strong or well equipped you become, it is important to realize that it can be an exercise in futility to try to reason with someone who would rather argue than maturely discuss scriptural truth. I have found that legalism leads to emotional immaturity. If you manage to corner a legalist, he often has one of two responses: volume or silence. If he has the upper hand, and is backed-up by numbers, organizational power, or political force, he will turn up the volume in the hope of intimidating you. The legalists have operated in this manner throughout history. You can see it clearly in their dealings with Jesus, Peter, Stephen, Paul, and anyone who refused to yield to their pressure. Legalists are often cowards but, never forget, they are mean cowards. They don't want to go it alone with someone who possesses true spiritual authority, so they plot and scheme until they have numbers or political or religious power behind them. Legalism killed Jesus, Stephen, Peter and Paul. See it for what it is: a slithering, cowardly thing. But give it the respect it deserves - the respect you would give a rattlesnake coiled at your feet.

That is not to say that you should not confront it. It is against the law to kill a rattlesnake where I live, but if I meet one on the path, I will quickly become a lawbreaker. If the opportunity presents itself, I will crush the head of every rattlesnake I meet. Why? I know if that rattlesnake bites a child there is a good chance the child will die. That is exactly how I feel about every legalistic, religious devil I encounter on the road. I want to take the puny thing by the throat and destroy its ability to cause harm or fear. We must develop the discernment to separate the legalistic person from the spirit attached to him. Our mission is not to hurt the person but to confront the spirit controlling or influencing him.

When you catch one alone, you will discover that legalistic religion lack of substance. There is no life or power underneath its hard bondage and oppressive rules. Jesus is the substance of authentic Christianity. Religion is just an empty shadow. The authority of religion and rules is always found wanting in the face of authority rooted in relationship. When you manage to force one to come out of the shadows, the legalist, depending on personality type, will respond in one of two ways: aggressively in order to intimidate, or passively like a hurting little child who wants to evoke pity. Many leaders, failing to understand the latter, have allowed legalists to slither away and come back to bite another day.

Jesus was not nice to legalism. It is enlightening to study His responses to it. He didn't even try to answer its questions. He was not polite to Pharisees, just as Paul was not nice to Judaizers – their Christian counterpart. He met their shallow, legalistic teachings with real authority. He didn't allow them unconfronted access into any realm where he had leadership responsibility. Read Galatians and you will be convinced that Paul absolutely refused to surrender an inch to it. Paul longed for peace but he determined that peace with this enemy would not come through a truce or treaty, only triumph. The kind of peace he opted for is the kind that comes when the battle is over, the dust has settled, and you are the last man standing: The kind you feel in the stillness when all your enemies lay motionless at your feet.

Does this sound a bit too strong for the polite, politically correct preachers of our day? Well, Paul wasn't like the seeker-sensitive, politically correct preachers of the modern church. He would have mutilated the "I love everybody and I'm not against anything" proponents of cheap grace. Paul was aware of something few American preachers in the modern church seem to understand; this world is a battleground, not a playground. He was a faithful soldier in the army of God. He had little patience for full-grown men who sit down and suck their thumbs at the first hint of pressure or persecution. He cried "Jesus" instead of "Mama." He didn't tolerate whining among members of his apostolic church planting teams. He was often heard repeating things that would turn the weak stomachs of many American preachers. Things like: *"And the God of peace shall bruise (crush) Satan under your feet shortly…" (Romans 16:20).* How can you talk about a God of peace crushing things – and how can you include both thoughts in the same sentence? One must wonder what some of the mice masquerading as men in the pulpits of America feel about such violent talk.

Paul often encouraged his disciples *to "fight the good fight of faith" and to "endure hardness as good soldiers of Jesus Christ"* (1 Timothy 6:12 and 2 Timothy 2:3). He spoke of *"wrestling against rulers of darkness and spiritual wickedness in high places" (Ephesians 6:12).* While enduring torture in a Roman prison under the insane emperor Nero, and waiting for martyrdom by beheading, he wrote to Timothy, *"I have fought a good fight"* (2 Timothy 4:7).

Did this guy even know how to say, "Ouch"? Polite, politically correct Christians often consider such men mean-spirited and hard. Credible Christians honor them as valiant soldiers in the greatest army that ever marched in this world. Paul was hard on everything that Jesus hated. He never backed up for the devil. He had real convictions and, for the honor and glory of God, he was ready to die for those convictions at any moment.

The church in America is full of big talkers who don't have the stomach for war. I have taken some of them on mission trips through the years. I remember a couple of big talking preachers who were the saddest of the lot. They weren't legalistic about many things, but they were about insistence on positive confession. They were still talking big faith at the nice hotels in the capital cities but they got quieter the deeper we went into the bush. "Sleep in a thatched hut? You must be kidding." Eat that? You must be out of your mind. "Mama! "Mama!" No wonder the Judaizers can operate unchallenged in so many of our churches. We have too few soldiers. And it takes real soldiers, who don't flee the field of battle at the first sight of blood, to combat an enemy as cold and cruel as a seasoned Judaizer.

Years ago I took one of these pseudo soldiers, who thought he had a spirit of adventure, deep into the jungle. He started whining as soon as we got out of the city. By his reaction, you would have thought the mosquitoes biting us were flying piranhas. After a long drive, followed by a long walk, we arrived at a village of thatched huts and were greeted by excited Indians. They were simple people who felt honored that we would visit them. (I felt honored to be with them) They prepared special dishes and treated us like kings. The first course was "chichcharrones" – something akin to pork rinds. They were a real delicacy among these people. The only problem was that they had been fried over a wood fire in grease that was not hot enough. Mr. Big Faith Talker looked at me and said, "You're not going to eat those are you?" I answered, "Yes, and with a smile on my face."

He refused the offer of a gourd full of them and I saw the hurt in the eyes of the toothless little Indian woman holding them out to him. I smiled back at her and took them enthusiastically. They didn't taste good and I was not accustomed to pork rinds going "squish, squish" as they were chewed, but by my smiling face the precious Indian women knew I was enjoying them. (I enjoyed their smiles much more than the food) Mr. Positive Confession lost all his faith. It just sprouted wings and flew away. He wouldn't eat anything so I ate everything. I explained it would be an offence to these precious people not to eat something they had prepared specially for honored guests, but his great faith just wasn't up to believing that if you eat or drink any deadly thing it won't harm you (Mark 16). He didn't eat until we got back to town the next day. He got sick. I felt great. I wouldn't want to fight an army of demons with soldiers like that watching my back.

The spirit connected to legalistic Pentecostalism carries legalism much farther than my faith and prosperity friend who was dogmatic about positive confession. It is domineering and divisive. It wants to control with rules, not serve with the love of a servant-leader. Those it can't control, it condemns. It also carries deception and seduction in its bag of ammo. Everyone who has been hurt by it must realize: This spirit wears many different faces. It is a modern manifestation of the hypocrisy Jesus condemned in the Pharisees, and Paul condemned in the Judaizers. I have said elsewhere in this book that the Judaizer spirit is a master of disguise. It will make you think you are on the same page until it has its religious claws in you. Be careful. You will sometimes feel confused when talking with someone bound by this conniving spirit. You are not simply processing words spoken by its proponents. You are being attacked by the spirit behind the words – and that spirit will claw your eyes out and feed them to the dogs that run with it, if given the opportunity.

Does the language seem a bit strong again? Read the Bible. Comfort loving preachers have lied to you. This world is a battleground, not a playground. Their ideas of fighting are nothing like those of real soldiers like David or Paul.

Legalists will fight, but on the wrong field of battle. They start wars with other Christians instead of fighting the forces of darkness for lost souls. Real warriors don't waste precious time playing silly little games or arguing with legalists who would rather make proselytes than win souls. Real soldiers recognize the danger of operating in enemy territory but attack anyway. Many of the soft, comfort loving "soldiers" of the modern faith movement fight harder to obtain material blessing than to win souls. The shallow, legalistic "soldiers" of Modalism waste their time fighting petty battles over bizarre doctrines that do not, in any way, threaten the enemy. The Apostle Paul fought another kind of battle; he wrestled with the powers of darkness to liberate lost souls. One soul was more valuable to him than all the comfort or wealth in the world.

Modern Christians are often like children on a playground getting hit by rocks coming from outside the fence. They don't see the devil throwing them so they assume that one of their playmates is the culprit. Before long, there is a full scale war taking place on the playground, and the devil is outside the fence laughing at the little children who think they are big, bad soldiers. Welcome to the world of strife and contention in the messed-up modern church.

Real soldiers of the Cross fight with a higher purpose and serve honorably with a greater sense of duty. They are not selfishly fighting for personal comfort or prosperity. They don't behave like little children on a playground. They viciously attack anything that threatens what they love. What the "softies" call sacrifice, they call privilege. They understand that the stakes are high. Real soldiers in God's army understand that they are fighting the forces of darkness for the souls of men. That is one of the reasons they are not nice to the enemy.

Are you wondering if you need a little more spiritual fortitude at this point? We should study the lives of the old warriors. It might help us to realize that many of the big mouthed faith talkers, and the legalistic Judaizers of our generation, are often "all hat and no cowboy." I know: I have seen many of them shrivel up under a hot sun in Africa and wilt like delicate little flowers when guns were pointed their way in Latin America. If you knew them like I know them, you wouldn't choose them to be your partner in a foxhole in the thick of battle. Talk is cheap. We desperately need more real soldiers who know what to do when they have a puny religious devil by the throat. We should learn from David: *"I have pursued mine enemies, and overtaken them: neither did I turn again till they were consumed. I have wounded them that they were not able to rise: they are fallen under my feet...thou hast also given me the necks of mine enemies; that I might destroy them that hate me...They cried but there was none to save them...Then did I beat them small as the dust before the wind: I did cast them out as the dirt in the streets..."* (Psalm 18:37-38, 40-42).

Lest some whining Pharisee suggest that I am advocating laying hands on them in an unscriptural manner, let me hasten to say that our warfare is spiritual. I am not trying to kill the Judaizers. I am after the spirits connected to them. I hate what they do to people. I hate the way they discourage zealous youth with their petty doctrines and unrealistic dress codes. I would welcome the opportunity to engage them in battle and beat them as small the dust before the wind. Beating these malign religious spirits down and watching them be blown away by the strong wind of God's violent love would be my idea of a great day. Don't shrink back when you find yourself locked into combat with them. They sound mean on the surface, but if you can catch one who is not reinforced by numbers, you will discover that there is not much there. Chances are, he is a lot of hat and not much cowboy.

Chapter Fourteen

Apostolic Revivalists or Apostolic Religionists?

Legalistic leaders are often harsh and domineering. They can be easily recognized. The polite, soft-spoken ones are a bit more subtle. They can infiltrate a group and not be recognized until they are in a position to make proselytes and do damage. There are some who operate this way without being fully cognizant of what they are doing. They don't realize that they are being manipulated and used by the spirit of the system they are attached to; but if you look back over their trail you will find that damage and division have followed them every step of the way.

Legalistic religious systems depend on co-dependent relationships. Their leaders know that some people are insecure and vulnerable. Such people can easily become controlled by rules, and the leaders who enforce them, because of their own insecurity. They live in bondage to an external code of conduct because their hearts have not been penetrated by love that writes God's laws on our hearts, nor empowered by grace that enables us to live from the inside out. An internal experience of grace and love which produces obedience is always preferable to outward striving to conform to an external code of conduct.

Religious spirits wear many masks. They wear the mask of weakness well. Watch legalistic believers with eyes wide open. Listen to their hollow laughter. Look at the oppressed expressions on their faces when you see them outside the church. They drag around as if the weight of the world is on their shoulders. The energy of life is absent. The adrenal rush that erupts when they press their doctrine is not the manifestation of life. They are energized by argument, not life. Many of the evangelists in the small world of Modalism call themselves "Apostolic Revivalists." "Apostolic Religionists" would be more fitting. Revival travels with life. There is no real life where legalism rules.

The spirits that energize these religionists have an innate ability to spot those who are wounded. One of their strategies is to come along side a wounded brother in order to establish a fleshly or emotional bond with him. The wounded brother is trapped before he realizes what it is that has sunk its "concerned" claws into him. One simple revelation will deliver him, but it is often difficult to lead even a new member of this religious club out of rules into revelation. They need to understand, *"Man looks at what is on the outside, but God looks on the heart"* (1 Samuel 16:7).

You may be thinking that I am hitting this too hard. You may even be wondering if I am doing the very thing I am condemning. Trust me; I am not. The difference is apples and oranges, night and day. There is no comparison. I don't live with the attitude that I have it right and everyone else has it wrong. I won't question your salvation if you disagree with my doctrine. But in the world of Apostolic Oneness and United Pentecostalism, you are not saved unless you believe and experience every tenet of their "Bible Standard of Salvation."

I have mentioned this elsewhere but it bears repeating. Do you realize that to say you believe this "Standard" is to say that everyone who has not been baptized with the proper formula, and who has not spoken in other tongues is shut out of heaven? It is truly small-brained religion that presumes to judge who is saved based on this dogmatic belief system. Judging by the standard of the Modalists, George Whitfield, Gladys Aylward, D. L. Moody, John Wesley, Charles Finney, Jonathan Edwards, Lottie Moon, Billy and Ruth Graham, David Wilkerson, and many of the greatest men and women of God in the history of the Church are not saved. This is not only mean religion: It is dumb religion. Jesus and Paul resisted it fiercely. Are we too polite to follow their example? Or are we just too fearful?

What would Paul say to these modern Judaizers who lay their heavy burdens on the backs of new believers? Probably something like, "What are you smoking, man," or maybe, "Get a life, dude." Or, to be more scripturally accurate, *"Are you really this foolish" (Galatians 3:3)?* His attitude toward modern legalists would be no different than the one he held in the first century: *"I would they were even cut off which trouble you" (Galatians 5:12).*

If, at this juncture you are thinking I am a bit sarcastic, or even mean-spirited I can only ask: "Do you think such ignorance deserves a more refined response?" How are we supposed to respond to such perversions of the glorious gospel of grace and liberty? I hope I can find the backbone to be as "mean-spirited" as Paul and Jesus. But the truth is, they were not mean-spirited at all. Their hearts were filled with love for both the legalists and their victims. But they hated the spirit driving the whole perverted system. We must not mistake the strength of holy love for mean spiritedness. A heart filled with the love of Christ also has room to hate what He hates – and Jesus hates hypocritical legalism which calls itself holiness.

The only holiness at many "Holiness Churches" is the name on the sign. They have forgotten that holiness is something of the heart, not outward conformity to exclusive doctrines, and strict codes of dress and behavior. The pressure of trying to live under such oppression is damaging in many ways. It will mess you up.

Rigid rules can lead to bizarre behavior. People who live under them need relief now and then. Over time, the only way to avoid blowing their lids is by regularly attending services where the air is filled with "Holy Ghost" excitement. But what is actually experienced in many of those meetings is not the moving of the Holy Ghost; it is a "soulish" release of emotion. Some realize it is all worked up in the flesh, but they jump in the water anyway. That is preferable to blowing your lid. If you are in bondage to rigid religious rules, you can feel like a hypocrite if you have any fun outside the church. The only relief for such a person is in a "Holy Ghost" blowout where weirdness often saturates the atmosphere. (The supernatural can be strange but it is never weird) What a miserable way to live. Such people become "Pentecostal junkies" and meetings become their fix.

Between meetings, they know nothing of the abundant life Jesus promised in John 10:10. The *"righteousness, peace, and joy in the Holy Ghost"* affirmed by Paul in Romans 14:17, is foreign to them outside the church; it can only be experienced in the right kind of meeting. They live in condemnation and constantly struggle with feelings of unworthiness. They develop dependence on meetings, and on those who know how to "lead" them, and that is exactly what the taskmasters of religion want. There is often a religious spirit behind the scenes driving the whole mess. Legalistic, religious spirits thrive in two kinds of atmospheres: an atmosphere of ritualistic "reverence" and an atmosphere of disorder and confusion.

A few months after my conversion, I encountered a trumpet playing street preacher from southern California. He invited me to meetings at a local holiness church where he was conducting a revival. He seemed cool, so I invited several recent converts and a few heathen to go with me. Somewhere between the shopping center and the church, that preacher lost all his "coolness." I think it was something in the atmosphere in the church building. The ten people who went with me were as traumatized as I had been when, as a nine year old, I attended church for the first time with a friend from school – a legalistic church which loved weirdness. My friends were uncomfortable the moment we entered. Some of the hardened "holiness" folks simply avoided us. Others greeted us with a longing look in their eyes that made me feel like prey ready to be pounced on.

The evangelist retired the trumpet a couple of minutes into the meeting and grabbed a microphone with the longest cord I had ever seen. (No cordless mikes in those days) He jumped from the platform and started running up and down the middle isle screaming, "Hallelujah! I feel the Holy Ghost." Things basically went downhill from there. When people started coming back to our pew to invite the "unshaved," long-haired men and the pants-wearing women to the altar, I took charge. Memories of childhood came to mind. I abruptly excused my group and we ran for the exit sign.

I didn't know much, but I knew enough to realize that true holiness did not conduct itself in such a chaotic and confusing manner. It took hours of discussion to calm down a couple of the people who had never been to church. They were as traumatized by the experience as I had been at a similar meeting in my childhood. It also became an issue of trust for some of them. I had told them how cool the evangelist was and convinced them to come to the meeting. I had egg on my face and they had a lot of questions. I wondered how many people had gone to churches like this and never returned. The discussion with that group of unbelievers and new believers made me realize what a serious issue this was.

I had, for the most part, dealt with my childhood experience in a similar church by just labeling the people who acted like that as "weird" and by deciding to stay away from them. I also remembered my decision as a nine year old to never go to church again and I realized that some of my friends, even though they were older, were in danger of making the same decision. I recalled how difficult it had been for my aunt to convince me to go to church with her, even though I realized she manifested none of the characteristics of the Christians at the holiness church I had attended in northern California. I also realized how important it was for me to take all the time necessary to talk with this impressionable group of youth and try to put their minds at ease. I finally succeeded by reminding those who had attended our meetings at Solid Rock Jesus Center that we never had meetings like that. The spirit of God moved and we experienced His power in our meetings. Sometimes it seemed strange because the supernatural is strange to the natural mind; but it never descended into weirdness. I wish every pastor could have a discussion like I did with those young people. They would come to understand, as I did, the dangers of legalistic Christianity and bizarre behavior in meetings.

The moving of the real Holy Spirit is not weird, unruly or chaotic. The Apostle Paul was quick to deal with the disorder in the Corinthian Church because he understood how such behavior could turn people off. We should remember his words to them in 1 Corinthians 14:33, *"For God is not the author of confusion, but of peace, as in all churches of the saints."*

I wondered how that evangelist could be so cool on the streets and so weird in a church building filled with religious people. Could it be religious spirits? What if such men, who are intelligent and anointed on the streets but weird in the religious atmosphere of legalistic churches became mature enough emotionally, and strong enough spiritually, to be who they are on the streets all the time? Is it possible that the real Holy Ghost would stand up and deal with some of the weirdness? He does specialize in bringing order out of chaos.

Chapter Fifteen

The Serpent Is Subtle

    To the pastor or leader who sees religious legalism for what it is, and yet allows it, Paul would warn; *"A little leaven leaveneth the whole lump"* (Galatians 5:9). Give a legalist a license to operate in your midst and soon others will join him. They do a poor job getting their own converts, but they are masters at messing with yours. Leave them alone, and soon their pervasive influence will contaminate the whole atmosphere. Allow it to continue unchallenged, and you will sentence yourself to religious excess and fleshly disruptions and never experience the order Paul contended for in I Corinthians 14:40.

    Is it wise to permit an unruly legalist, who seems to be incapable of winning souls himself, come in to mess with those under our care? Paul didn't think so. We should wonder if there is not something wrong in a man who, instead of going out to win his own converts, wants to set up camp on our grounds, or hang out in our churches, and subversively attempt to make proselytes of those we have brought to Jesus.

    There must be something seriously wrong with his gospel. Why is he not able to get his own followers? And if he is not able to do so, why should we afford him leadership status and give him access to ours? Perhaps your assignment, instead of giving him a platform for ministry, is to help him determine if he is truly a leader. It's a no brainer. All he has to do to discover if he is a leader is to look over his shoulder. Is anybody following? If not, it is time for him to wake up and smell the coffee. If he has no followers, he is not a leader. That being the case, he should not be allowed to come into the midst of those following someone else and try to act like something he is not. We must find the wisdom and strength to tell such men to go get their own converts.

I was once witnessing to a drug addict whom I had prayed for many times. He was really close to opening his heart to Jesus. I had spent about an hour talking and reading scripture to him. He said with tears, "I know I can't go on like this. If Jesus can do for me what he did for you, I want to receive him." I was so excited. I asked him to bow his head and begin to pray. At that very moment, a United Pentecostal guy came by and said, "You won't tell him the whole truth, will you, Sutton?" People who are thinking clearly understand that truth should be presented one step at a time. Lead the person to Jesus. Take him to a few meetings. Encourage him to be baptized and to begin seeking the fullness of the Spirit. You don't back your religious dump truck up to his driveway and dump the whole load at one time.

The guy who interrupted me went on to say, "Are you going to tell him he has to speak in other tongues?" I couldn't believe it. A drug addict was standing before the cross ready to pray to receive Jesus but when he heard the reference to tongues, he said, "Are you one of them. I don't want anything to do with this." I was never able to get him to open up again.

I would like to ask every hard-working pastor, who often does the work of an evangelist, this question: Do you want converts who received Jesus at your altars to be told by Mr. Pentecostal Legalist that they are not saved until they speak with other tongues? If that is truly what you want, or even what you don't want but allow, then welcome to bondage, frustration, and smallness. If that is not what you want, then it might be wise to suggest to Mr. Modalist that he go find his own followers? If you continue giving him access, even if he seems to be a nice guy, his little leaven will eventually contaminate the whole loaf of bread.

Jesus fought legalism throughout His ministry; Paul fought it everywhere he travelled. May God give us the presence of mind to fight it too. May God give us the discernment to recognize it – whether it walks in wearing a condemning smirk or a congenial smile. Remember, Judas marked Jesus for death with a kiss. The devil is a master of disguise. He walks in behind many different faces. Those he can't dominate, he attempts to deceive. The serpent is subtle. He sometimes hides his poison behind the face of one believed to be a friend. He uses "concerned" brothers who endear themselves to you during a time of great difficulty, or after you have been wounded. They encourage you in the hard time in order to establish a bond that will give future access. Some of them sincerely want to help but, if they are attached to a religious system that keeps people in bondage, it is possible that they are being used by a spirit which wants to bring you under the same bondage.

The serpent is subtle. We need to ask the Holy Spirit to give us discernment to recognize the devil – no matter what face he is wearing. Authority and power to defeat him will follow the discernment. We should deal with the devil wherever we meet him – in the church or in the world. There is no need for a blood-bought believer to back up for him: *"Submit your selves therefore to God. Resist the devil, and he will flee from you"* (James 4:7). *"Ye are of God, little children, and have overcome them: because greater is he that is in you, than he that is in the world"* (1 John 4:4).

Chapter Sixteen

The Left Foot of Fellowship

I was a hippie, saved in the early days of the Jesus Movement. When I was born again, I had long hair, a beard and a gold ring in my left ear. I was quickly introduced to the difference between loving believers and legalistic Judaizers. I thank God for the loving ones who left me alone long enough to let the Holy Spirit work on me.

I was given the "left foot of fellowship" at several churches. I regret not taking all the money offered for haircuts by legalistic Christians at those churches.. I also received offers of help to purchase a new wardrobe. What was up with that? I had two pair of jeans, four faded t-shirts, several other really cool shirts and two jackets. I won't take time tell you about the encouragement this new Christian got over the gold earring. Wow, man! Can't we all just love one another? I share some of my experience here to let you, dear reader, understand that I know something from personal experience about mean religion.

I have now, after forty years of ministry, contended with Judaizers all over the world. In the early days, they focused on getting me shorn and shaved. As time went on, my influence in the Jesus Movement grew. Bored Christian youth, some of whom had left legalistic churches, started coming to my meetings along with many who had never attended church. I established two Jesus Centers south of St. Louis and hundreds came from miles around. About two hundred were still coming on Friday and Saturday nights when I released the ministry to co-workers and moved to establish a Christian community and drug rehab ministry.

In those early days of the Jesus Movement, some insecure pastors accused me of pulling the youth out of their churches. I reminded them that most had already left before I came along, but that didn't help. Legalistic pastors were downright mean. Two of them labeled me a spiritual "Pied Piper" who deceived youth and taught them to talk in other tongues. Christians from a church I had attended briefly began floating the rumor that I hadn't truly been converted, that my Christianity was just a front, and that I was dealing drugs out of the backroom of the storefront where we held our meetings. Eventually, most of them left me alone; but not the legalists. The worst attacks came from the United Pentecostal Church. Man, those guys were mean.

They were convinced that many of the young people in my meetings had come from their churches. The truth is, most of them were new converts or backsliders who had recently returned to the Lord. But that didn't stop the attacks. Members from one of the larger United Pentecostal Churches in the area seemed to show up wherever I was. They interrupted me when they found me giving out tracts and preaching on the streets. They butted in on conversations when I was witnessing one on one. They said "intelligent" things in the presence of the unsaved like: "He won't tell you the whole truth. He will tell you that Jesus loves you and will forgive you, but he won't tell you about the Holy Ghost. He won't tell you that you have to speak in tongues to be saved."

Once, two of their leaders came to one of our meetings, stood up during the worship, and began to rebuke me. After stopping them, I asked the worship leader to sing another song. She chose "In the Name of Jesus". They left at the exact moment we sang the line "demons will have to flee". Hmm… kind of makes you wonder, doesn't it?

I know it is provocative to write such things but, hey, somebody needs to do it. Jesus deliberately provoked the Pharisees, and the bottom line is that these are true stories. The things I am telling you actually happened. Provocation can sometimes be a good thing. There are reasons why Jesus deliberately provoked the Pharisees by breaking their rules, hanging out with sinners, calling them snakes, etc. – and it wasn't because He was a contentious person. He provoked them to make them step out into the open. He refused to let them hide in the shadows. He forced them into the light. Devils like to do their work in the darkness. Pharisees like to stack the deck before they play their cards. They find strength in numbers. Jesus forced them to come out in the open so he could expose their hypocrisy.

Had religious legalism not caused their brains to misfire, they would have had the presence of mind to just leave Jesus and His revolutionary followers alone. Gamaliel, a respected leader among the Pharisees, tried to get them to do just that. Remember what he told them after the Resurrection when the Pharisees lamented that even though Jesus was gone, His disciples were still preaching the Gospel and, horror of horrors, they acted and sounded a lot like their Master? Gamaliel's advice: *"Leave them alone. If this thing is of God, you can't stop it. If it is not, it will come to nothing"* (Acts 5:34-38).

Jesus quickly dispensed with the sophomoric questions of the Pharisees. He confounded them with words of wisdom and knowledge, and sent them away stuttering. His disciples had the same anointing after Pentecost. Jesus made the Pharisees look like the hypocrites He knew them to be – and He did it in front of the crowds. He provoked them and ridiculed them. Why? He understood better than anyone the danger of the corrupting influence of their belief and practice. He wanted His followers to remember how He had rebuked them soundly so they would not be deceived by their subtlety when He was no longer there to personally deal with them.

Chapter Seventeen

A Reputation in Hell

The shadow of religion causes no fear in the regions of darkness. The substance of real relationship with the risen Christ causes hell's foundations to tremble. The devil fears the resurrection life of Jesus. Religion is empty and powerless in the spiritual realm. It is restricted to the physical realm of religious organization and political power. The authority of relationship can do business in both realms. John the Baptist preached in power that the Pharisees had never experienced. He refused to follow their protocol and his dress code was not up to their holy standard. They wanted to do away with this troublemaker but a certain look in his eyes, and a certain tone in his voice, caused them to walk a wide path around him.

He disturbed them even more by declaring that One with greater power was coming on his heels: Greater power than this rugged prophet who had wrecked religion, shamed its hypocritical leaders, and stirred the entire nation? Those words spoken to the Pharisees on the banks of the Jordan River were an indictment of powerless religion that stands to this day: *"I indeed baptize you with water unto repentance: but he that cometh after me is mightier than I, whose shoes I am not worthy to bear: he shall baptize you with the Holy Ghost, and with fire" (Matthew 3:11).*

Jesus operated exactly as John said he would. The religious world was thrown into turmoil long before He turned over their tables and ran their money-mongers out of the temple. The legalists knew that their power was being challenged, and that their miserable lifestyles were in jeopardy, the first time He opened His mouth. They didn't understand true spiritual authority but they felt its effect and they saw its fruit.

"And it came to pass, when Jesus had ended these sayings, the people were astonished at his doctrine: For he taught them as one having authority, and not as the scribes" (Matthew 7:28-29).

" And when he was come into his own country, he taught them in their synagogue, insomuch that they were astonished, and said, Whence hath this man this wisdom, and these mighty works" (Matthew 13:54)?

"And Jesus returned in the power of the Spirit into Galilee: and there went out a fame of him through all the region round about…and he went into the synagogue on the Sabbath Day, and stood up to read. And there was delivered unto him the book of the prophet Esaias. And when he had opened the book, he found

the place where it was written, The Spirit of the Lord is upon me, because he hath anointed me to preach the gospel to the poor; he hath sent me to heal the brokenhearted, to preach deliverance to the captives, and recovering of sight to the blind, to set at liberty them that are bruised, to preach the acceptable year of the Lord. And he closed the book and he gave it again to the minister, and sat down. And the eyes of all them that were in the synagogue were fastened on him. And he began to say unto them, This day is this scripture fulfilled in your ears" (Luke 4:14-21).

Anyone hearing these words who had an ounce of discernment knew that this was a declaration of war. This Rabbi was different. It sounded to some as though he had plans to dismantle the whole religious system they had worked so hard to build. Their power was being threatened. The revolution had begun. The powerless legalists stood on the sidelines, amazed at the miracles; but their pride prevented them from admitting that someone with greater authority was in their midst.

Legalism restricts the flow of life that contains miracle working power. Legalism is "letter of the law" religion. It always produces death. When people recognize the difference between it and the true gospel which always produces life, they begin asking questions - questions that infuriate the proud purveyors of religious bondage. They don't want to admit that their lives are shallow and their words are void of power, so they continue in their ignorance and try to control people with petty rules. That is why relationship always trumps religion: It is filled with life and power. Religion is dead because it loves petty rules and functions under the letter of the law which frustrates the power of grace. There was something much different about Jesus and everyone knew it.

"And they were astonished at his doctrine: for he taught them as one that had authority and not as the scribes. And there was in their synagogue a man with an unclean spirit; and he cried out, saying, Let us alone; what have we to do with thee, thou Jesus of Nazareth? Art thou come to destroy us? I know thee who thou art, the Holy One of God. And Jesus rebuked him, saying, Hold thy peace and come out of him. And when the unclean spirit had torn him, and cried with a loud voice, he came out of him. And they were all amazed, insomuch that they questioned among themselves, saying, what new thing is this? What new doctrine is this? For with authority commandeth he even the unclean spirits, and they do obey him" (Mark 1:22-27).

The poor legalists didn't get it; they still don't. The devil fears life, but he crawls in bed with religion. He sits on the front row at its meetings and never has an uncomfortable moment. He uses it when he needs to and mocks it when he wants to. The legalists I have dealt with don't have the power to deal with the puniest demon in town, but their dead doctrine has so chilled their hearts and so dulled their minds, they don't even realize their miserable condition. They are impotent because they live by the letter of the law but run from the higher law of life in Christ Jesus. The law brings death; the Spirit gives life. They have no life because they are married to religion. There is no life and, therefore, no power apart from vital relationship with Jesus.

Acts 19:11-16 graphically demonstrates the absence of real spiritual authority or power in legalistic religion. It also reveals its ignorance. *"And God wrought special miracles by the hands of Paul: So that from his body were brought unto the sick handkerchiefs or aprons, and the disease departed from them, and the evil spirits went out of them. Then certain of the vagabond Jews, exorcists, took upon them to call over them which had evil spirits the name of the Lord Jesus, saying, We adjure you by Jesus whom Paul preacheth. And there were seven sons of one Sceva, a Jew and chief of the priests, which did so. And the evil spirit answered and said, Jesus I know, and Paul I know; but who are you? And the man in whom the evil spirit was leaped on them, and prevailed against them, so that they fled out of that house naked and wounded."*

Paul cared little about what the legalistic religionists thought of him, but he did work hard to establish a reputation in hell. When Paul arrived, every demon in the area knew he was in town. They felt him walk into their atmosphere. They worked hard to make his visit a short one. They dreaded to see him wake up each morning because he tormented them with every waking moment. Demons mocked the religious crowd. They played with them, charged the atmosphere of their meetings with weirdness, and drove them into the harsh bondage of petty rules and rituals.

It was different when Paul was around. When he spoke the atmosphere was disturbed and demons listened. When the legalists spoke, the demons laughed. Can you imagine the turmoil caused by Paul's encounter with the religious exorcists in Ephesus? Powerless religious hypocrites were exposed; the whole city was in an uproar. Demons trembled as they watched their servants pile up books on witchcraft and curious black arts in the city square. They must have had convulsions when their former followers danced around the biggest bonfire in the history of Ephesus. It was just another normal day in the life of a man who turned from the deadness and impotence of legalistic religion to embrace the authority and power of real relationship with Jesus.

Are the legalists of our day any different? Do they possess real power and authority? Is it true spiritual power or are they just like the Judaizers that intimidated and controlled people with exclusive doctrine and petty rules? What does the puniest devil in town think of their harsh religion? Is he impressed by its rigid rules and strict dress codes? If the ignorance of legalistic religion has not numbed our brains, we will receive revelation from this graphic encounter in Ephesus. Think about it: A skinny heathen man filled with puny demons chased seven religious leaders down the street in front of the whole town.

Paul had a different experience. Demonized people throughout the city gathered up books on witchcraft and black arts and brought them to Paul's bonfire in the city square. Religious imitators must have moments when they face the truth about what they are doing - moments when the absence of power is so evident that they must admit, at least to themselves, that there is no reality in their dead religion. If it is truly the power of God operating, it would not be necessary to strive to work it up in a meeting. A man's authority is in the word he speaks. If he has the real thing, the real Holy Spirit will be released when he opens his mouth. He won't have to play religious games and strive to create an atmosphere where flesh and emotion are mistaken for the moving of the Holy Spirit.

There is a day of reckoning somewhere down the road for every leader who is not authentic. If we fail to heed the warnings and refuse to repent of religious pride, we are going to one day meet a puny little demon that will beat and strip us in front of our deluded followers and chase us naked down Main Street screaming, "Jesus we know, and Paul we know, but who are you? It is better to face that question before you run into that puny demon. If you discover you are not who you thought you were, there is a solution: *"Humble yourselves under the mighty hand of God...." "But he giveth more grace. Wherefore he saith, God resisteth the proud, but giveth grace unto the humble. Submit yourselves therefore to God. Resist the devil, and he will flee from you"* (1 Peter 5:6 and James 4:6-7).

I have watched proud religious leaders, who talked big and loud in America, reduced to a whisper in a dark field in Africa. I have watched them choke on their big words, in numerous situations, when the pressure was on in different nations. It is one thing to preach boldly in America; it is another thing to do so in a hostile environment.

I was a member of a delegation of preachers when doors began to open in Russia in the early 1990's. Each of us spoke in different churches at night and conducted seminars together at a Moscow hotel during the day. One of the preachers was very insistent on positive confession. He was also legalistic and arrogant: arrogant enough to criticize preachers who had remained faithful under years of communist persecution and oppression. Their faith was much more refined and developed than mine or any other member of our team. I knew that but "Mr. Big Faith Talker" was in too much religious fog to perceive it. He corrected them for their "negative confessions" and berated them for lack of faith. He boldly challenged them to rise up and lead the charge to bury the body of Lenin which had been on display for many years in a museum in Red Square. He admonished them to rise up in faith and authority. He rebuked them for allowing the devil of communism to continue intimidating them after the Iron Curtain had come down.

He had no idea that several things meaner than communism were still roaming the streets: Former KGB agents who had been transformed overnight into free enterprise entrepreneurs, the Russian Mafia, and even worse, a vicious religious spirit that still had an army of Russian Orthodox priests who were ready to assert their superiority over leaders of the new revival taking the former Soviet Union by storm. Some of the young Russian Christians were really impressed by his great faith – but not all of them. They felt the emptiness of his big words and made some interesting plans for him.

These young Russian preachers were no joke. A couple weeks before our visit, a preacher had told them that, with the coming of revival, they should be healing the sick and raising the dead. Two of them went to a nearby funeral home and got the body of a dead friend out of his coffin. They dumped the corpse on the platform mid-sermon and said, "Show us how to do it." To his credit, he tried but was unsuccessful. The big-mouth in our delegation didn't know about that experience. He had no way of knowing that these young preachers had become a bit skeptical of big talkers from America.

Later, on the night of his great oration, the "KGB" visited the wing of the hotel where the American preachers were residing. They banged on our doors and ordered, "Come into the hall with your passports." I heard the commotion as they got closer to my room. Finally, they were banging on my door and commanding me to open it and come out. They got louder and louder because I refused to open the door. That has been my policy late at night all over the world.

The next morning at breakfast everybody was disturbed. A lot of faith had been lost as a result of the late night visit by the "KGB." No one was talking about great exploits of faith. But I noticed that some of the young Russian preachers were really enjoying themselves that morning, especially two of the former KGB agents who had brought their uniforms to the conference.

Young Russian preachers told me about Mr. Big Mouth who stood trembling in the hallway the night before. He was wearing nothing but his funny looking boxer shorts and stuttering as he tried to answer the questions of the "KGB" agents. They told me the whole story because, according to them, I was the only preacher in the American delegation who refused to open the door. I had simply ignored them at first but when they kept banging on the door I yelled back, "If you are the KGB, go get a master key from the front desk and open the door yourselves, or just kick it down. But if you do come in here, you better be the KGB."

Can you believe it? Faith-filled, American preachers opened their doors late at night in a Moscow hotel and stood fearfully against the wall, dressed in funny pajamas and boxer shorts, obediently answering every question asked by the "KGB" agents. Impressive, isn't it? It makes one think that talk might be cheap. The Russian preachers, whose faith had been refined in the fire of communist oppression, already knew that. They could discern whether a preacher had anything underneath his words. The big faith preacher proved their theory. Word travelled fast. That's why my seminar was packed but only a few who were unaware of the events of the night before went to hear big-mouth. (I realize that some who read this account will say, "That is joking and jesting which is unseemly." Maybe it is but it resulted in much better teachings for the rest of the conference).

Some men who talk big faith in America become alarmed to learn that you can't call 911 when a demon disrupts your meeting somewhere else in the world. Others wouldn't dare enter a building without security or an army of armor bearers. Some preachers who talk big in the security of their sanctuaries at home lose their train of thought, and stutter a lot, in front of a massive African crowd shot through with demonized people living in fear of witchcraft. Talk is cheap: Religious talk is cheaper.

You can't establish a reputation in hell by talking big faith or observing strict codes of conduct and dress. Devils are not impressed with empty words nor the narrow doctrinal systems legalists pretend to live by. Devils fear only one thing – the life of Jesus. There is no life in religion. It would be wise to trade religion for a real relationship with the living Christ before you run into a witch doctor on a dark night in Africa. They do not fear the shadow of religion. If you are one who moves in the shadows, you will one day be standing in the hall wearing nothing but your boxer shorts.

The Apostle Paul traded the legalism of the shadow of religion for the power of the substance of real relationship with Jesus. If you are one who endeavors to impress others by your strict adherence to rules and dress codes, if you are more concerned about the length of someone's hair, or whether a woman dares to wear pants, make up or jewelry than you are about what is in their hearts, religion has reduced you to an empty shell. You will encounter, around some bend in the road, a puny demon who knows there is nothing underneath all the talk. He will know that a hat does not a cowboy make.

The power of religion against the power of hell is revealed in Acts 19:13-20: One skinny demon possessed man chased seven big healthy religious leaders down the street shouting, *"Who are you."* If you are ever called upon by a demon to answer that question, it is time to run. Modern legalism is as void of real power as Sceva's religion. It is all shadow and no substance: all hat and no cowboy, all talk and no power. Religion talks and imposes rules. Authentic Christianity acts and backs up its words with spiritual power rooted in relationship, not rules. *"And I, brethren, when I came to you, came not with excellency of speech or of wisdom, declaring unto you the testimony of God. For I determined not to know anything among you, save Jesus Christ, and him crucified. And I was with you in weakness, and in fear, and in much trembling."*

(Hypocritical, religious legalists would never admit to such weakness. Paul acknowledged it without blinking). *"And my speech and my preaching were not with enticing words of man's wisdom, but in demonstration of the Spirit and of power: That your faith should not stand in the wisdom of men but in the power of God"* (1 Corinthians 2:1-5).

If you one day go to Africa to help me with a mass crusade, I won't care whether you are clean-shaven, whether your hair is over your ears or touching your collar. I won't care whether you preach in long or short sleeves, wear a tie or don't wear a tie. If you are going into war with me, I just want to know if you love Jesus in sincerity, if you are carrying religion or walking in relationship, and if you know how to pray. And I am not as concerned about your reputation among men as I am about whether you have established one in hell. I don't want to face demons on a dark field late at night and hear one say, "What's up, Ron? Who is that with you? If I take you to Africa, here is what I really want to learn before leaving the security of our American sanctuaries: Does anything in hell know who you are?

Chapter Eighteen

Violent Love

Every godly shepherd has a responsibility before God to protect those who look to him for leadership. Leaders who take this responsibility seriously are alert to spiritual danger. They confront those who come into their midst with false doctrine or a wrong spirit. Some respond positively to correction, stay and become a blessing to the church. But others will come who are dangerous. Some will be goats. One goat can disturb the peace of an entire flock of sheep. Goats tend to be stubborn and exhibit aggressive behavior. The pastor, who tries to ignore them and avoid confronting them, does so to the detriment of the entire flock.

Wolves in sheep's clothing are even more dangerous. Leaders must be vigilant to watch for them. Jesus warned, *"Beware of false prophets, which come to you in sheep's clothing, but inwardly they are ravening wolves"* (Matthew 7:15). Loving pastors sometimes forget that what a person appears to be outwardly may be a lot different than what he truly is on the inside. If something that looks like a sheep growls or bites, you don't need discernment to figure out what he is. Don't leave your followers unprotected. Deal with the wolves. The dangers to the flock posed by wolves were a great concern to all the apostles of the New Testament Church. Paul's heartfelt words to the Ephesian elders should serve as a reminder to us of the seriousness of this problem:

"Take heed therefore unto yourselves and to all the flock, over which the Holy Ghost has made you overseers, to feed the church of God, which he hath purchased with his own blood. For I know this, that after my departing shall grievous wolves enter in among you, not sparing the flock. Also of your own selves shall men arise, speaking perverse things, to draw away disciples after them. Therefore watch, and remember, that by the space of three years I ceased not to warn everyone night and day with tears" (Acts 20:28-31). Paul's words must be heeded by every true shepherd. To fail to warn and protect the flock from wolves, and other harmful or dangerous influences, is a dereliction of duty.

Wolves should be dealt with quickly and firmly. They must be killed or driven away. Wolves cannot be given access to the sheep. We need more leaders who are willing to kill a wolf in sheep's clothing. Real love has the stomach for war. The Bible is filled with accounts of violent acts of love. The prophet Samuel had a heart of love, but his kind of love was different than that of many polite, modern leaders. It could be tough and even violent when necessary. Samuel's dealings with the evil

Agag, spared by a compromised leader, left no doubt about the violence of his love. It also reveals the attitude of a loving God toward leaders who refuse to deal with evil they have been commanded to destroy. Few modern pastors have the stomach to even think about some of these Old Testament accounts. They are too squeamish to even say the word "sin" much less cut it to pieces in front of a crowd. God is loving. The Bible tells us that He takes no pleasure in the death of the wicked. He is not legalistic but He does not like compromise and he can be firm in dealing with evil.

"Thus saith the Lord of hosts, I remember that which Amalek did to Israel. Now go and smite Amalek, and utterly destroy all that about they have, and spare them not (Saul had no question concerning his assignment. Agag was to be destroyed)... And Saul smote the Amalekites...and he took Agag the king of the Amalekites alive...so Saul and the people spared Agag... Then came the word of the Lord unto Samuel, saying, It repenteth me that I have set up Saul to be king: for he is turned back from following me, and hath not performed my commandments. And it grieved Samuel; and he cried unto the Lord all night... Then said Samuel, Bring ye hither to me Agag the king of the Amalekites. And Agag came unto him delicately. And Agag said, Surely the bitterness of death is past. And Samuel said, As thy sword hath made women childless,

so shall thy mother be childless among women. And Samuel hewed Agag in pieces before the Lord in Gilgal" (1 Samuel 15: 3, 7-11, 32-33).

Does this story leave any question about the willingness of a loving God, and the willingness of his prophet, to deal violently with evil? This is the violent side of love about which polite, mild-mannered leaders in the modern church know so little. I am certainly not advocating the literal killing of wolves or cutting people to ribbons. I know our warfare is not against flesh and blood today. I realize that the battle is spiritual. What I am suggesting is that we need leaders who have enough discernment to see what is hiding under the sheep's clothing, and enough spiritual strength to deal with the spirit that came in with it.

Saul had been commanded by the word of the Lord through Samuel to destroy all of the Amalekites. This seems like a harsh command coming from a God of love, but such actions were sometimes necessary to contain the spread of evil on the earth. When Saul failed to carry the assignment to completion, Samuel took charge. He knew that allowing someone as evil as Agag to live would result in great harm to God's people in the future.

Can you imagine what our lives would be like today had there not been a Winston Churchill, who knew that compromise with someone as evil as Hitler was out of the question? Churchill met evil with great determination and force even though he knew that victory would come at great cost; but he knew the cost of not dealing with the evil would be greater. The same is true for the pastor who apathetically ignores the activity of legalists among the flock. His failure to deal forcefully with it will result in believers being wounded, weighted down with bondage, or even lost. The frustration of legalism sends many away from our churches disheartened and discouraged, never to return. Legalists are often like the Judaizers of Paul's day. Many are wolves in sheep's clothing that must be driven away by courageous shepherds. Legalism is mean religion; it must be met at the door with violent love.

Chapter Nineteen

The Foundation of Mean Religion

Bad doctrine is the foundation of mean religion. It may seem a bit extreme to cite an example, as I did in the last chapter, of an Old Testament prophet cutting sin to pieces when dealing with the subject of mean religion. Few would dare think that religion could be so mean as to require the angry response of such violent love. The truth is, religion can be so mean that it will cause most polite, mild-mannered preachers of the modern era to run for cover; the truth is that it is meaner than most want to believe. We are dealing with a belief system that is standing on legalism and division. The expression of that belief system, in daily practice, is the epitome of mean religion in action.

Why is bad doctrine the foundation of mean religion? Because what you believe influences how you think and affects what you do. Misconception and misrepresentation of the Godhead stand behind the legalism of religious systems like Apostolic Oneness and United Pentecostal groups. The "Jesus Only" view produces division and strife. It serves a strict God who imposes and enforces rigid doctrinal positions and petty rules of dress and conduct. Its "Bible Standard of Salvation" puts some of the greatest men and women of God in the history of the Church in hell. The Modalists broke from Orthodox Christianity 1900 years after the Church was born in Jerusalem. Their narrow "Jesus Only" view should be labeled heresy by every serious student of Scripture and Church history.

These dogmatic legalists refuse to entertain the possibility that there is plurality in the Godhead or that the concept of "Oneness" has to do with the miracle of holy love enjoyed by God the Father, Son and Holy Spirit. A lot is lost by failing to embrace the plurality of the Godhead. It moves the believer's heart just to ponder how Three can abide together in complete oneness - oneness that expresses itself in passionate love in a holy atmosphere of perfect unity and harmony. We cannot fathom the depths of the eternal love experienced by the Father, Son and Holy Spirit. We can only bow to God's revelation of Himself to man, and rejoice that He so freely shares His love with us.

Modalism essentially denies salvation by grace and justification by faith. It is a works based, letter of the law religion that condemns anything that doesn't agree with it. It is driven by the spirit of the Judaizers. Modalists add unscriptural requirements to salvation by grace through faith, and bury new believers under the rubbish of man-made religious doctrines and rules. They discount the clear teaching of John 3:16 and a large body of Scripture that adds weight to the doctrine of simple faith which, if left alone, will produce the obedience they try to force on people with man-made doctrines. The obedience produced by faith does not look or act like the coerced obedience of mean religion. The obedience of faith brings real love and freedom, not condemnation and bondage. Love leads; religion drives. May God help us to clearly understand the difference.

Many evangelical leaders get it and challenge the perversions of Modalism. Why can't the Pentecostals do the same and police themselves? Why are we so reticent to treat it like Jesus and Paul did? This mean religion puts men like David Wilkerson, Charles Stanley and Billy Graham in hell. What kind of person would suggest that Billy Graham is destined for hell because, as far as the Modalists know, he has neither been baptized in Jesus' name nor has he spoken in other tongues? Are we required by love to tolerate something that destroys people we love? Shouldn't more level-headed Pentecostal leaders find enough spiritual fortitude to call it by its first name: Heresy?

Religious legalism is shallow and lacks true spiritual authority. It prefers to sneak up behind its target. It operates covertly and tries to set a trap for its prey. It uses surprise attacks and relies on the strength of numbers whenever possible.

Religious legalists who find their security behind a title, or in a position, like to contrive their plots secretly. It can never succeed without a Judas to do its dirty work.

But legalism becomes a cowering, cringing little thing when forced out of its comfort zone to face someone with true authority like Jesus or Paul. Jesus quickly dispensed with questions small-brained Pharisees thought were clever and difficult. They were left embarrassed and looking bewildered time and time again when they made the mistake of facing Jesus out in the open; but the watching crowds went away amazed at His wisdom and authority.

There is darkness and dullness in the brains of legalists. Their minds are so tightly wrapped around their narrow belief system that they leave no opening where light can get in. They are set in their ways and refuse to be confused with the facts – even if the facts are well supported by scripture. That is why the legalist is always at a disadvantage in an open confrontation with someone whose mental faculties are energized by the light of life. The authority of title or position is always found wanting in the face of authority that operates out of relationship. There is a power in spiritual life that is feared by the devil and his demonic hordes.

The conflict is for life. The resurrection life of Jesus prevailed over the power of hell and death. The devil fears the life of Jesus. That is the reason he attempts to smother it with religion. That is why he works so hard to restrict or restrain it. He doesn't want another Pentecost. He hates revival because revival releases life. That's why he infiltrates churches which still move in the Spirit. That is why he likes to make a dried up legalist appear to be a wise, elder brother to a younger believer who still has a little zeal. He is after the precious life.

Legalists never seem to get it. Religion smothers life. Its formal systems of rules and rituals destroy it. There is no energy in religion because there is no life. Life is produced, and reproduced, in the passion and energy of spontaneous relationship. Religion is an organized system held together by adherence to man-made doctrines, rituals and rules. Real Christianity is a living organism, a vibrant relational community bound together by the fellowship of a shared Life. Lifeless legalists despise the liberty of believers who possess it. Legalism restricts the flow of life. We should endeavor to help those bound by it but, if possible, we should protect new believers from their influence. Pastors would be wise not to give them recognition before the congregation. Religious spirits love to be noticed. The flesh likes to stand in front of a crowd. Give them ground to stand on and soon they will be rising to testify and running to lay hands on people in your altars. Listen with discernment and you will know that their words are empty. Watch those they pray for as they rise from the altar and you will know that their hands are heavy. Leave the legalists alone and they will ruin every revival that breaks out in your midst.

Chapter Twenty

Loose Lips

In this chapter I am going to share some personal experiences with modern Pharisees. I share them not to vent my feelings, but with the hope that they will help you understand the damage proponents of mean religion can cause. The first is an experience from early in ministry with an uneducated man who thought he knew everything. In 1974, we established a Christian community which had a drug rehabilitation ministry with about forty people in the program. The recovering drug addicts in the program were barely able to function. Simply getting up and getting dressed was a challenge. Showing up for morning devotions "clothed and in their right minds" was a major accomplishment. My staff understood their struggle and gave them a little space until they were able to function and "get it together."

But there was a proud Pharisee in the church we were connected to who knew more than our staff. He was a retired farmer from Minnesota who knew little or nothing about drug addiction, but he was convinced that he knew just what the people in our program needed. He often criticized me to my face and behind my back. He continually "helped" without being asked. He constantly criticized my staff and took the liberty to correct those to whom we were ministering. He was convinced that their biggest problem was laziness and he knew exactly how to fix it. That old farmer, now become Bible student, was certain that he knew how to better run the program. When we didn't implement his suggestions he became offended and started slandering us at every opportunity.

When I confronted him the loose-lipped legalist suddenly transformed into a pitiful, wounded believer. His voice changed and he spoke with doleful expression and a whine in his voice. He walked away from me shaking his head in disbelief, not understanding why we wouldn't take his advice.

I was surprised, about two weeks later, to see him show up at our elders' meeting. I didn't know that prior to the meeting he had managed to evoke pity from several of them. He had convinced them that I was wrong for telling him to stay away from the recovering drug addicts in my care. The meeting was not pretty. Attack after attack came at me from my concerned fellow elders. They were determined to help me see how I had wounded the poor Pharisee but they seemed to have little concern for the "poor" recovering drug addicts I had denied him access to.

One elder who, through most of the meeting, remained unconvinced that I was mean-spirited finally went over to the "enemy's" side when that sly old Pharisee suddenly repented and begged my forgiveness. And how he repented! He crawled from the other side of the circle, placed his hands on my faded jeans, looked up at me and said, "Please forgive me, brother. I have wronged you."

I responded by saying, "I forgive you, but your repentance is not sincere and at least two of us in this room know it." Excuse me for saying, "All hell broke out in that room-full of elders." I was rebuked and called nearly everything except a loving leader; but I knew what I was dealing with. I had met this devil before. I didn't grow up in church. I came off the streets. It normally doesn't take spiritual discernment for me to recognize a hypocrite. To survive in the world I came from required identifying those who are not what they appear to be.

The leading elder was convinced that the Pharisee had a loving heart and, I suppose, the ability to reform wayward women: So much so, that a troubled young woman was placed in his home about a week after the elders' meeting. Two weeks later, I found myself at an unscheduled elders' meeting with the old Pharisee, his wife, and the young woman in attendance. It was soon revealed that the poor, wounded brother started visiting the bed of the needy, wayward woman two days after she moved in with them. He didn't repent until he was found out. But his loving wife, and some of the elders, were moved with pity for the old snake and convinced of the sincerity of his "godly" sorrow.

Pharisees can put on a good act when they are found out. They know how to wear a lot of different faces. We could avoid a lot of trouble by remembering how Jesus and Paul dealt with them. We must learn to stand firm in love and not allow our emotions to be manipulated by an insincere apology. We would be wise to remember that the pitiful, whining little thing standing in front of us often converts back into a loose-lipped Pharisee the moment our back is turned. Don't let a pitiful expression trying to hide phony repentance fool you. Even a whining, little snake can diffuse lethal poison.

At this point you may be thinking, "Man, this guy has had a lot of controversy." I would have to plead "guilty as charged." My only defense would be to say that I am in good company. The Apostle Paul had more controversy than I could handle in two lifetimes. Most people who refuse to give Judaizers a pass do have a few battles along the journey. But those who try to live with integrity should not avoid confrontation. The only hope for those afflicted with legalism is truth spoken in love and firmness by someone who is not intimidated by them.

I have discovered that legalistic leaders are often loose-lipped. They are capable of doing you great damage. Legalism is mean and malicious. It may try to hurt you even though you have never had a conflict with it.

In the 1980's I was done great damage by another proud Pharisee. He was more loose-lipped than the farmer, and more intelligent. His words and actions were calculated and deliberate. I was taken off guard by his attack because I thought we were friends; we had never had a conflict. The damage he did me is literally incalculable. I have since learned that he has damaged many others by slander which had no basis in truth. It is sad that such men are so seldom confronted. I did confront him but I underestimated the damage that his diarrhea of the mouth would do me over the course of many years. Because of his sin, doors were closed that were never again opened.

The slander of a Pharisee can hurt you more than you can imagine. Don't make the mistake I did by underestimating the potential for danger and damage because you think people who know you would never believe it. Legalists are often afflicted with a weird combination of insecurity and pride. Insecurity and pride become more dangerous when they are connected to the loose tongue of a loud-mouth who is full of himself. I will never know how many relationships were affected, or how much support was lost, because of his unwarranted slander.

He visited Costa Rica, where my wife and I were missionaries in the early 1980's. I never saw him, nor did I talk with him while he was there. I learned the details later – after the damage was done. While there he asked another missionary, whom I didn't know very well, "How is the orphanage Ron is building coming along?" The missionary responded, "What orphanage. I don't know anything about an orphanage." San Jose with its suburbs, the city in which we were based, had a population of over a million. I was on one side of the city; the missionary "loose-lips" talked to was on the other side. He didn't know half of what I was doing and I knew little about what he was doing. He did have my phone number though. I was only ten kilometers and one phone call away. "Loose-lips" could have called me. He could have paid me a friendly visit and asked questions of me personally. But he didn't.

Had he asked me, I would have gladly taken him to the muddy slum where my dear friend Edgar Chacon and I were preaching the gospel to the poor and endeavoring to show them love in word and deed. I could have taken him to the building sight. I could have shown him the road built with picks and shovels. I could have shown him the concrete being mixed in a wheelbarrow, and the blocks being made by hand, one by one, in wood forms.

It would have been a real missionary experience for him. I could have explained to him that things sometimes move a little more slowly in Latin America. But I didn't have the opportunity to do any of that, because he didn't bother to consult me. He just returned to St. Louis and told several churches and individuals that supported me that I wasn't building an orphanage. Some of them told others, who in turn told others. A friend of "Loose-Lips," who occasionally leaves his beautiful home and comfortable church in America to take short-term missions trips to exotic places, zealously helped to spread the false report (He had ulterior motives which I won't elaborate on here. Suffice it to say that much support I once received, he now enjoys). By the time I got wind of this travesty, damage control was nearly impossible. A respected leader who knew me well, and knew about my work in Costa Rica, sent out a letter to pastors and churches in the St. Louis region. It helped but a lot of damage had already been done and, unfortunately, much of it was irreparable.

After finishing a mass crusade, I immediately flew to St. Louis and began contacting supporters. I visited one businessman who, for a couple of years, had been donating five-thousand-dollars a month to our ministry. "Loose Lips" knew him and had already talked to him. Oh, the damage one loose tongue can do! What if that businessman would have continued supporting us? How much is five-thousand-dollars a month from 1983 to 2014? And that's just one person. I have no idea how much one false report has actually cost me.

Am I bitter? No. I try to remember people like Joseph and become "better, not bitter." You have to forgive in order to move on with God. A blessing can sometimes be extracted from the pain of bitter experiences if we find the grace to forgive. God can use them to develop us and accelerate the growth process in our lives. I went on in ministry and God supplied generously. An outpouring of unexpected new support helped me continue our international projects as well as a home for unwed mothers in the U.S.

I hope you never have to suffer from the actions of someone like "Loose-Lips" but, just in case you do have the privilege, don't hold your breath until he repents. Guys like him seldom do. They go on running their mouths, never stopping to consider the amount of damage caused by their actions. I think that it would be great if gossips, especially malicious slanderers, could be dealt with more effectively. Wouldn't it be a better world if more Christians believed that, "Those who gossip, and those who listen, should both be hung: One by the ear, the other by the tongue?" Someday they will be.

I have probably devoted too much space to "Loose-Lips," but I have done so in the hope that something like this never happens to you. If it does, I urge you to take action as quickly as you can. The pride of legalism produces mean religion. Proud leaders who are impressed with themselves often what we call windbags. They are so full of hot air they can cause a virtual tsunami in your ministry. Don't be as naïve as I was; don't underestimate the damage their brand of mean religion can do. I wonder how many orphanages and Bible schools have not been built, how many evangelistic crusades have not been conducted, how many gospel tracts have not been printed, how many dedicated servants of God have suffered, because of proud, loose-tongued people like this?

Before moving on, I should tell you about my last encounter with "Loose Lips." I didn't let him slither away unconfronted. I later saw him at a large church in St. Louis (which, in another lifetime, supported me very generously). I got straight to the point and said, "I have been told that you are talking about me and saying some very disturbing things. I don't want to believe what I am being told without hearing it from you." His response says it all: "Oh, I know how it is, brother. We all have to rob Peter to pay Paul sometimes."

But my question for him didn't have anything to do with Peter or Paul. I simply looked him in the eyes and asked, "Why didn't you talk to me? I was only a phone call away." He muttered some sort of unintelligible response and found an excuse to leave. He didn't even have enough integrity to repent to my face. He still has a good reputation (among those who don't truly know him) but what is the worth of reputation without character? Eternity will tell.

I urge you to be careful of such men but don't allow yourself to become bitter toward them; that would only hurt you more. Move forward in faith. God is able to restore what has been stolen from you. He can even give you grace to pity and pray for people like "Loose Lips" who do you so much damage. You can pray with love and mercy in your heart because you know that what the devil meant for evil, God can turn to good – that what the devil meant to destroy you, God can use to develop you. If you have trouble believing this, ask Joseph. He knows, better than anyone, that it is true. *"But as for you, ye thought evil against me; but God meant it unto good, to bring to pass, as it is this day, to save much people alive"* (Genesis 50:20)

There have been many others, not mentioned in this book, who tried to hurt or hinder me, trip me up or do me in through the course of forty years of ministry. I will share one more experience here that I hope will help you be more alert to the spiritual dangers associated with mean religion. We must not underestimate its potential to harm us. I dealt with witchcraft and many witch doctors in Africa from 1986 to 2007; nothing I met in Africa was any meaner than the mean religion I have described in this book.

I had the honor of working with one of the great men of God of our day, B.H. Clendennen, founder of The School of Christ International which eventually had schools in over one hundred nations. After spending some time with me in Zambia, he asked me to direct the school for the continent of Africa.

A few years later, an evangelist who resented my relationship with Brother Clendennen, and the trust and support he gave me, tried to do me in. His actions cost me support and friends, but fortunately Brother Clendennen was not affected. He called to assure me that I still had his confidence, and I had the honor of serving under his leadership until I contracted malaria in Mali, West Africa several years later.

The evangelist still has a good reputation among those who don't truly know him, but again, what is reputation without character? The scales of eternity will balance everything. That legalistic evangelist was jealous and his character was too weak to deal with it. Pharisees often blow their cover and manifest the behaviors of mean religion when someone else obtains favor they have tried hard to get for themselves. Though I had never done anything whatsoever to harm him, he went for my jugular. Had he succeeded he would have left me lying in the ditch, bleeding and bruised.

I share this experience to be able to say, "Be on guard against surprise attacks." If you are anointed, if you are a threat, the enemy will target you. Mean religion caused Jesus and Paul a lot of grief; if you are truly anointed by God, it will cause you trouble also. The darkness coming on the earth will require us to be "wise as serpents and innocent as doves." Men like "Loose Lips" and evangelists with diarrhea of the mouth will hurt you, but don't give in to discouragement. Legalistic Christians will slander you and try to cut the ground out from under you, but if you keep your heart with all diligence God will make a way for you. Character will outlast reputation.

Eventually, you will be able to see the hand of God in some of the things you thought were going to do you in. Like Joseph, you will live to see his goodness come out of the treachery of unscrupulous men (Genesis 50). Like David, you will live to see God's goodness in the land of the living (Psalm 27).

I have reached the place where I can actually thank God for enemies I once thought to be friends. They have helped me. They drove me deeper into God. They forced me to grow. Their attacks made me stronger. The pain they caused made me tougher but somehow, by God's amazing grace, it also made my heart more tender. God taught me through Joseph's example that I could become better, not bitter. I have to thank God for those who have caused me grief and trouble because, the truth is, they helped me become more like Jesus.

By God's grace, I have survived much more than the attacks of mean religion. I have experienced great blessing, and great opposition, throughout the world. The devil has not ignored me and I take that as a great compliment. A demonized woman once screamed over and over, "You satan! You satan! I smiled and said, "Thank You." It is my firm conviction that the worst insult Satan can pay you is to ignore you. I am blessed. He has not ignored me from the earliest days of ministry.

I have survived serious accidents, power-tripping Sandinista soldiers, crazy Hare Krishna devotees, angry Muslims, corrupt "Christian" leaders, priests who ordered my death, pimps upset that we had rescued some of their victims, zombies, ju-ju and voo doo curses, a junkie who contracted to kill me for a measly one-hundred-dollars, etc. (I thought I should have been worth more than that, but he was desperate for dope) In the end, the reprobate who hired him came on his own and held me at gunpoint for over an hour. I prayed and rebuked him in Jesus name over and over. He later told several people that he tried to pull the trigger numerous times but something had it locked up. The dummy probably had the safety on, but I like to think that I was supernaturally saved by angelic intervention.

The truth is, no anointed servant of the Lord would last a day without His covering and protection. We will be here until God is finished with us. It doesn't matter if the devil uses a warlock or a demonized Pharisee to try to do us in. God is able to deliver us and keep us until He calls us home. I have survived the curses of many witch doctors and Satan worshippers. The fearful little people sent by witch doctors throughout Africa couldn't bring themselves to do harm to the crusade preacher as ordered. One said I had some kind of force field around me that he couldn't penetrate.

If I had my choice, I would be in heaven already. But if by staying on earth I can reach even one more soul, then let me stay. I have come back from pneumonia so serious that my Costa Rican friends called my wife, who was at home in the USA, and told her to book a flight immediately. I had pushed myself with a high fever for seven days, trying to finish a crusade and leaders' conference. I finally collapsed and later woke up to hear the doctor saying, in Spanish he didn't know I understood, "He is a dead man." When my beautiful wife arrived and walked into the room, I thought I was having a vision. I have also survived hepatitis, Lyme's disease and multiple bouts with malaria.

My last attack of malaria took me to the mat. I had been running on high octane jet fuel for several years. Hundreds of thousands of dollars in support had come in year after year. I was conducting several international crusades and leadership conferences each year. Ten schools and two orphanages had been started in various African nations. While preaching in Mali, West Africa, which has a population that is ninety-seven percent Muslim, I arranged to conduct a crusade in Timbuktu – the first Muslim holy city. I was on top of the world. But suddenly I was brought down by the bite of a puny malaria infested mosquito. What witchdoctors and mean religion had not been able to do, a puny mosquito did. It knocked me off my high horse. I lost a lot but I now view much of the painful ordeal as a blessing. It humbled me and I needed to be humbled. The devil wanted me to feel sorry for myself, but instead I feel blessed. Humility has great value. With God's help, I will rise again and serve Him with a better spirit than before.

Chapter Twenty-One

He Couldn't See My Heart for My Hair

The following story sounds like fiction but it is true. In my early days of ministry, I was blessed with regular visits from legalists. Two busloads of them showed up to crash one of our meetings at Solid Rock Jesus Center in 1974. The Saturday night they came, nearly two hundred young people were packed into the storefront building we rented in House Springs, Missouri. The group of about sixty small-brained legalists got off the buses, marched into the building and actually tried to take over the meeting. They were determined to straighten out my "false doctrine" at any cost.

Their youth pastor stood at the back and his clean-cut, properly dressed followers started passing out tracts during our worship service. This was United Pentecostalism at its best - going into all the world to make proselytes out of somebody else's converts. The tracts said things like, "To be saved you must be baptized in Jesus name and speak in other tongues" (Just the sort of thing a crowd of pot smokers, speed freaks, bikers, drug dealers and recently converted Jesus People needed to hear).

I politely asked the pastor to halt the disruptive activity, retrieve the tracts, and join us for the rest of the meeting. He didn't pay any attention to me. His little religious brain didn't allow for the possibility that someone who looked like me could be saved, much less lead a meeting. I was "unshaved" so he assumed I had to be unsaved. I had long hair and he couldn't see past my hair to my heart. He had no intention of listening to me. He was on a mission to help my poor followers see the glorious truth of his bondage producing, legalistic religion. He began to shout, "Don't let him deceive you. He knows the truth but he won't preach it."

Wow! This was getting a little weird. I had to restrain some of the crowd. Several of the recently converted bikers were ready to lay hands on him in an unscriptural manner. They hadn't been saved long enough to know it wasn't nice to beat up preachers – not even rude, legalistic ones. The pastor went on, "He won't tell you that you need the Holy Ghost so somebody has to."

He was beginning to get on my nerves. I told him again to put up the tracts and join the meeting but he refused. He left me no choice. I asked the worship leader to grab his twelve string and get ready to lead some more singing. I instructed everyone in attendance to watch me and do exactly what I did. I took one of his tracts (which condemned to hell those who had not spoken in other tongues or been baptized in Jesus name), walked to the big trash can at the back of the crowd and threw it in. Each person who had been given one did the same. That was a good thing; the tracts covered up the pot, pills, and paraphernalia that had earlier been thrown in the can. In the early days of the Jesus Movement, it was not unusual for repentant youth to throw drugs away after leaving the altar – and sometimes spontaneously during the course of a meeting.

Rev. Religious still wouldn't leave. He left me no choice. I snatched the box from his hands and dumped its contents in the trash can. He seemed a bit off balance, but he still wouldn't sit down or leave. He cleared his throat a couple of times and started trying to preach. I finally had to help him out the door and his bewildered, clean-cut disciples followed him to the buses. Unbelievable! But it actually happened on a Saturday night in the summer of 1974 at Solid Rock Jesus Center in House Springs, Missouri.

I share these crazy encounters because I really want you to believe that I do know something from personal experience about mean religion. Legalism gets a little crazy when it meets somebody who defies it. It does some weird, below- the- belt kind of stuff when people won't come under it, or give space to it.

I will never forget the first missionary I heard preach a couple of months after my conversion. I arrived at the church early and sat on the left side in the front row. During the next half-hour the building filled up, but nobody else sat in my row. I assumed they weren't as excited as I was about hearing a missionary from Africa. About half way through the song service, I realized that not one of the loving Christians in that church had greeted or welcomed me. It also dawned on me that I was the only bearded, long-hair in the house. A little farther along, during a rare moment of lucidity, I realized that nobody else was wearing faded jeans and a T-shirt. Man, I was really under-dressed for this joyous occasion.

My discomfort dissipated the moment the missionary stepped up to the pulpit. My excitement heightened when he said, "I felt led to preach on the Great Commission this morning."

Far out, man! I was all about the Great Commission. I dreamed of being a missionary myself someday. But I guess that pious preacher didn't see that in me. The next thing I heard was, "But when I see this young man sitting here on the front row, I feel the Holy Ghost leading me to go a different direction." I thought, "Wow! This guy must really be led of the Spirit." But the next hour was a bit weird. The missionary began by saying, "Turn with me in your Bibles to Luke 19:10 and stand for the reading of God's word." He continued, *"For the Son of man is come to seek and save that which was lost."*

Before going on, let me assure you that what you are about to read actually happened. It is the truth, the whole truth (as clearly as I can recollect it), so help me God. The next thing I heard was the missionary referring to me again. It didn't take a rocket scientist to figure out the direction this thing was heading.

The missionary continued, "Brothers and sisters, when I look at this young man I am reminded of all that is wrong in America today. I feel the liberty in this moment to paraphrase our text. I believe it could also be said that *"Jesus came to seek and to "SHAVE" that which was lost."* I laughed. That was great, really funny. Then I came out of the fog. No one else was laughing! This guy was as serious as a heart attack. He spent the entire sermon on me. I remember lines from his sermon like, *"Does not nature itself teach that it is a shame for a man to have long hair"* (1 Corinthians 11:14)? "All these hippies want to do is lay around, smoke pot and cohabitate. We need to help them find the money to pay for a haircut and a shave; don't let them infect the youth in our churches, etc."

What a waste of everybody's time. He spent the entire sermon on me. He could have saved his breath, and everybody else's time. I already knew that without Jesus I was the worthless piece of trash he had preached about for the last hour. Do you know what is sad about this true story? His legalistic, religious brain couldn't get wrapped around the possibility that someone who looked and dressed like me could truly be saved. He didn't have a clue that we had the same Father and that I was also a member of the royal family. His doctrine prevented him from even entertaining the possibility that someone who looked like me could be saved. He couldn't fathom how I could be "unshaved" but not unsaved.

Do you know what else is sad about this story? Similar versions were repeated in legalistic churches all over the country and many of the targets of this pathetic brand of preaching didn't survive. A lot of people just like me, recently born-again and filled with love for Jesus, thought His followers would love us too. We were naïve. We knew nothing about mean religion and strict dress codes. We didn't know about legalistic religious systems which perverted the gospel and added a boat-load of man-made doctrines and rules to it. I can only wonder how many excited new believers left a meeting like that never to return to church.

Do you know what else is sad about this story? Legalism blinded that missionary and kept him from perceiving in the Spirit what was sitting in front of him. He didn't know because he couldn't see my heart for my hair. He couldn't see a heart beating with love and desire to serve Jesus. He couldn't see a heart burning with passion to reach the lost at any cost. He didn't know that the "unshaved" piece of trash, who became the subject of his sermon, was destined to become a missionary, conduct mass crusades, start Bible schools, orphanages, a home for unwed mothers, a drug rehab program, and plant churches. He didn't know that the "unshaved" piece of trash would write books, study materials, and gospel tracts that would be translated into numerous languages and circulate around the world. He didn't know that the "hippie" sitting alone on the front row would go on to minister in sixty nations.

Do you know what else he didn't know? That "unshaved hippie" went home to his little cabin, got down on his knees, and prayed for him. Do you know why he didn't know? Because he forgot that *"man looks on the outward appearance but God looks on the heart"* (1 Samuel 16:7) His doctrine put me in hell because I had long hair and a beard. If you could see me now, forty years after I survived that sermon, you would know what I think about his mean religion and the legalism that rules it. My hair got shorter over time but, after all these years, I am still "UNSHAVED."

Chapter Twenty Two

Religion or Revolution?

My last battle with malaria left me horribly hammered. I honestly thought it was all over. After months of struggle with no improvement, I made some of the most painful decisions of my life. I resigned as director of the School of Christ in Africa. I made one phone call that cost me nearly two-hundred thousand dollars a year. I released the last church I had founded to my son Ryan, who shouldered the responsibility like a veteran soldier of the cross and moved forward in faith. I shut down the mission organization my wife and I founded in 1976 and distributed the assets to mission-minded churches and ministries.

My mantra in the face of every challenge for over thirty years had been, "Forward ever, Backward never!" Now it was all I could do to get out of a chair and walk across the room. The devil I had fought all over the world was dancing on my head. Puny demons that I had formerly walked on were beating me to death. Every sin and failure of my life came before my face day after day. The devil really didn't need to beat me down. I was doing a good job of it myself.

I have shared my weakness and struggle because I want to encourage anyone else who knows what it is to feel hopeless – whether it is due to frustration from religious legalism and bondage, or from difficult circumstances in life. You can recover. With Jesus, there is always hope. Never give up. You may feel alone but you are not. The God who loves you has promised to never leave you or forsake you. He is greater than all your problems and He is committed to help you.

God "fleshed out" His love for me by working through a few key people. My family was patient with me and refused to believe that I wasn't coming back. My wife and children demonstrated amazing faith and true agape love. A friend from Dallas called me regularly and encouraged me more than he will ever know this side of heaven. Although many of those who should have helped me – the ones I had helped the most through the years – acted like I had leprosy and avoided me, God sent help from unexpected places. One young preacher, who I had helped through the years, loved me like Jesus and refused to let me sit down and feel sorry for myself. He constantly called me, came to get me out of my recliner and made me do things I didn't want to do. He continually reminded me that the only way out was to get up in faith. He looked me in the eye countless times and said, "I know who you are and you are not the person I hear saying I can't do this."

I was convinced that I could not go on and was ready to give up. I really felt like sitting in the corner, sucking my thumb and crying "Mama." But I knew that wouldn't do any good and the brother showing me so much love was a real soldier. I doubt that he knows how to say "Ouch," but he is filled with the love of Jesus and is as tender as he is tough. He took me to churches and stood me up to preach. He took me to tent revivals and introduced me like I was the greatest thing since sliced bread. Sometimes when I preached I saw a blurry crowd through blood-shot, burning eyes and was barely able to stand.

He refused to let me hide in my weakness and amazingly, in spite of my weakness, he never stopped respecting me. He honored me when I felt like there was nothing left in me to honor. And he continually said to me by phone and to my face, "Speak the Word and you will get up and walk out of this by faith." I don't know if I would have made it without him. Religion doesn't do what he did for me. Nothing but love rooted in relationship acts like that. One day, I started speaking the Word, got up and started walking by faith. Now when a devil gets in my way, I am again saying what I said from the early days of ministry: "Forward ever, Backward never! I am coming through in Jesus' name."

I want to say it again: Religion didn't bring me back. It left me bleeding by the side of the road. Legalist believers didn't give the mosquito that infected me with malaria any credit. They launched a campaign to convince anyone who would listen that my sin had brought this on me. I felt as if Job's comforters had come back from the dead. Their mean religion robbed them of all compassion. Because I had confronted them and had warned others to be careful of their doctrine, which condemned everyone who didn't believe, behave and dress as they did, they insisted that I was just reaping what I had sown.

Those Pharisees left me bleeding by the side of the road; but "Good Samaritans" who had love that was rooted in relationship rescued me. My faith faltered but God's love was always there. Jesus was tender, loving and merciful all the while I was condemning myself. Grace is amazing. Legalistic religion would have finished what that malaria infested mosquito started; but liberating relationship with a loving Savior healed and delivered me. At the end of faith I found hope and hope kept me, even when my feeble faith was faltering.

The powers of darkness hit my family hard while I was in a weakened state. It seemed that a hedge came down and hell came at all of us with force and fury. I wouldn't go through the trial that began with a blood-sucking, malaria infested mosquito again if you offered me a million dollars. But it would cost you a lot more than that to buy the benefits of this long trial from me. My faith has been sorely tested and my only hope is that it will come forth like gold refined in the fire. I met the mercy of God on a deeper level than I thought possible and I experienced an intimacy with the Savior I love that is worth more to me than all the pleasures and riches in this world. And I discovered that when I am too weak to go on, I can go on anyway because His grace is sufficient for me, and His strength is made perfect in my weakness.

I am still fighting to come back. I am still shaken and things that were once easy are now often very difficult. But I remain determined to emerge from this long struggle to serve God with a heart of love for the hurting. I want to live with a heart of gratitude in the service of the King and count it a privilege to serve Him in any capacity. I want to rise again, dead to selfish ambition, but gloriously alive with desire to please the One Who loved me and *"washed me from my sins in His own blood"* (Revelation 1:5).

I learned during the darkest period of forty years of walking with God that religion is powerless to help you when you are in deep waters. Instead of helping, it will try to push you back under. It will weigh you down with condemnation when you are struggling to keep your head above water. That is why I am bold to be politically incorrect and say that I spit on mean, legalistic religion. I hope I can start a spitting contest and recruit an army of real soldiers who share my disdain.

Love hates legalism. Jesus was not nice to the Pharisees. Paul was not nice to the Judaizers. Jesus came to start a revolution, not a religion. Religion will lock you up in a prison of ridiculous dress codes, moronic doctrines, and petty rules. The radical love of relationship with a revolutionary called Jesus will liberate you and lift you into the heights of another world. Do you want death in legalistic religion or life in a liberating revolution? It's a no brainer, man; spit on the religion and join the revolution.